TYNESIDE

CITY AND COUNTY HISTORIES

General Editor: Lionel Munby

Department of Extra-Mural Studies,
University of Cambridge
Editor of *The Local Historian*

In preparation

CORNWALL	Lawrence S. Snell
DERBYSHIRE	John Heath
DORSET	J. H. Bettey
DURHAM	B. K. Roberts
GLAMORGAN	John Davies
LANCASHIRE	J. D. Marshall
NOTTINGHAM	Alan Rogers
THE POTTERIES	Michael Greenslade and Denis Stuart
SOMERSET	R. W. Dunning
TEESSIDE	Barry Harrison

CITY AND COUNTY HISTORIES

TYNESIDE

C. M. FRASER PhD FRHistS
K. EMSLEY MA LLM

DAVID & CHARLES
Newton Abbot

In Memory of
Clifford Briggs Emsley
and
William Hector Fraser

Set in 12pt on 13pt Bembo
and printed in Great Britain
by Latimer Trend & Company Ltd Plymouth
for David & Charles (Holdings) Limited
South Devon House Newton Abbot Devon

CONTENTS

LIST OF ILLUSTRATIONS

Chapter 1   THE TOPOGRAPHY OF
                TYNESIDE

TYNESIDE is becoming standardised into yet another English subdivision. It has resisted the process manfully, and the dialect still defies imitation by the comedians of club-land. Some children are still bi-lingual, speaking 'polite' in public but 'Geordie' in the home; but the international pop-culture has poured over most, and long-haired, trousered teenagers walk the streets as in any other conurbation. The Newcastle Civic Centre is built in the fashionable cosmopolitan style—'a secular cathedral'. The new hotels and office-blocks are concrete and glass abstractions. There are the usual developers' shopping precincts, and elaborate motor-ways with underpasses and fly-overs. Tower blocks of flats punctuate the skyline, as in many another town. The acres of workers' houses, three-roomed flats on two floors, are being replaced with three-roomed flats on four to ten floors. The inter-war council estates age ungracefully. Anonymous semi-detached villas crowd along the roads—here in grid-formation and there in planned irregularity. Chinese 'take-away' restaurants mushroom. Before the pressures of international conformity obliterate spontaneous regionalism, let us investigate Tyneside, the home of the 'Geordie'.

It must be admitted that the origins of the nickname 'Geordie' have been forgotten. The 'pitmen', who worked the coal synonymous with Tyneside, were called 'Geordies'; it is said because they used the safety lamp devised by George Stephenson, of *Rocket* fame, rather than the lamp invented by Sir Humphrey Davy. Still earlier, Tyneside had stood firm for George I against the Old Pretender. Either or neither fact may provide the explanation.

The Tyne valley is pre-glacial. In its present form, it represents a

9

drift-choked basin, where solid rock emerges only at certain points. It was the presence of two such ridges of stone which enabled the Romans to bridge the river at *Pons Aelius*, now Newcastle upon Tyne; and the road systems of Northumberland and Durham converge on this point. The river Tyne has its main sources in the Cheviot hills and in the Pennines. The North and South Tyne unite at Warden near Hexham, some thirty miles from the river mouth, and enter the coal measures by Wylam. The area known as Tyneside begins a little west of Newburn, and extends seventeen miles downstream, to Tynemouth and South Shields. This represents the river jurisdiction of the corporation of Newcastle over the tideway, which was estimated to extend from Ryton to the river mouth. It is now the responsibility of the Port of Tyne Authority. From Newburn the river banks are lined, almost continuously, by wharves, docks, quays, factories, ship-yards and power stations as far as Tynemouth on the north bank and South Shields on the south.

The present-day scene bears little resemblance to the beautiful river of the ancient kingdom of Northumbria, described as a tortuous, shallow stream, full of sand shoals, which impeded its flow from Walker downstream to Spar Hawk, at the harbour entrance. Even at Newcastle, the river was said to have been fordable at low tide, and small schooners lay stranded at the quayside. J. M. Carmichael, in a series of Tyneside paintings, shows its changing moods, whirling past Bill Point before spreading sluggishly over the marshes of Jarrow Slake. From thence the river made another sharp turn around Whitehill Point, through the narrows, and over more sandbanks into the North Sea. The original harbour was nothing more than an inlet on the north bank of the river, flanked to the south by the Herd Sand and to the east by the dangerous Black Midden rocks. Every winter brought its large share of wrecks, as there were no piers to quell the angry sea-breakers. The only evidence of commerce was to be seen in the little wooden quays which lay alongside the river at North Shields, Hayhole, Wallsend and Elswick. Jarrow was still a small village; and the tiny industrial undertakings at Elswick gave no inkling of the huge munitions empire at Armstrongs that was to emerge here. Moored to buoys

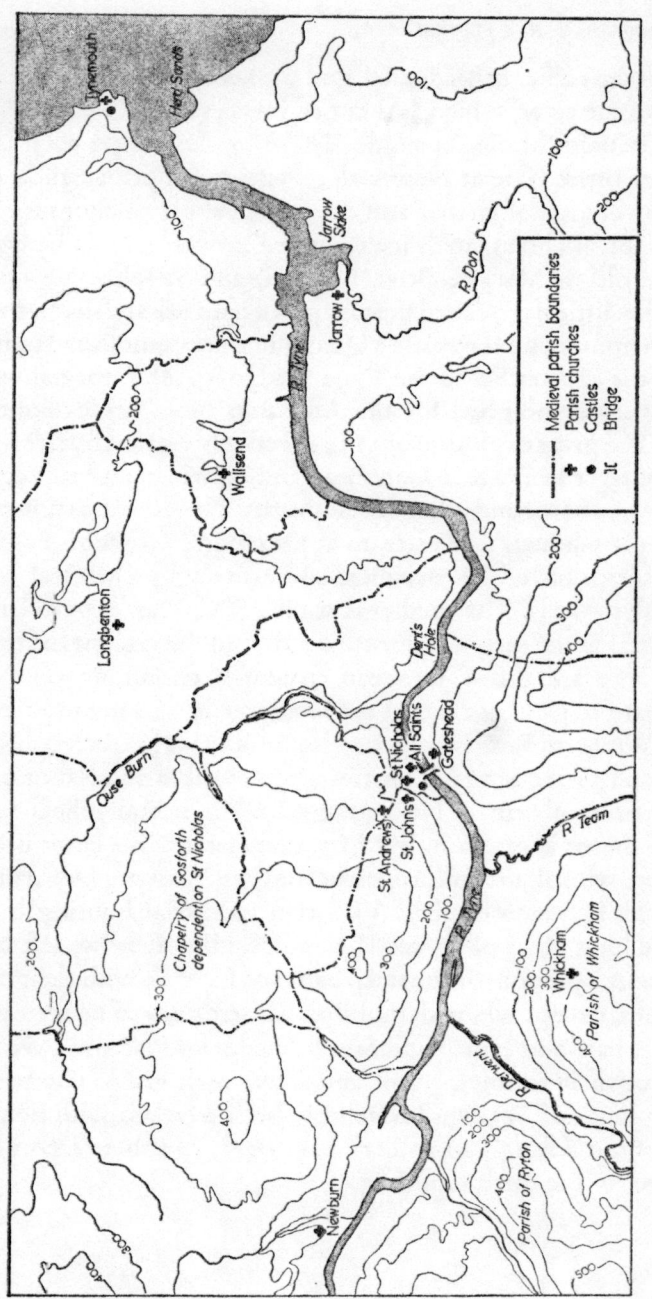

Fig 1 Tyneside

in groups the collier brigs floated, and the keel-boats plied slowly up and down the river, which was famed for its salmon.

Little remains of old Tyneside. There are landmarks such as the castle and Black Gate at Newcastle, Tynemouth priory and castle, the Saxon church of Jarrow and the medieval parish churches of St Andrew, St Nicholas (with its 'crowned' tower, said to be copied from the old St Mary le Bow, London) and St John, Newcastle. Otherwise, little has escaped the ravages of hard use and ill treatment. Jacobean houses on Newcastle's Quayside were demolished to make way for the approaches to the Tyne bridge (1928). Georgian warehouses were demolished for the All Saints office re-development nearby. The great explosion of 1854 effectively cleared by fire a long stretch of river frontage in Gateshead and Newcastle for subsequent factory, warehouse and office development. The sites of seventeenth-century glass-houses downstream at Ouseburn, Howdon Pans and South Shields have been occupied successively by chemical works and by ship-yards. The medieval walls of Newcastle were largely demolished in the early nineteenth century in the interests of traffic-flow. There are a few Jacobean frontages remaining on Newcastle's Sandhill and pockets of old Georgian houses in Summerhill, behind Westgate Road; Regency houses in Camp Terrace, North Shields and Front Street, Tynemouth; as well as the elaborate re-development of central Newcastle with shops and offices in the 1830s in the style of Nash, but fifty years later. This latter is to be preserved, with all the enthusiasm of the City Planning Department. Elsewhere Tyneside displays Victorian industrial housing by the acre; the long rows of Byker Hill looking like furrows left by an iron-master's plough, or the steep banks of Elswick with their clinging houses, except where demolition has left scars of broken walls. The river banks of North and South Shields and Jarrow have been cleared of their teaming slums and sown with grass. The few remaining fields of Wallsend have now been overlaid with housing, now that the Rising Sun colliery has closed, and there seems to be no danger of the earth subsiding.

TRINITY HOUSE

Tyneside has always been willing to sacrifice the picturesque for the profitable; not least so with its river. Newcastle corporation assumed responsibility for conservation of the Tyne in the fifteenth century, and imposed tolls and river dues nominally for the upkeep of its shipping channel. It was abetted by the Society of Masters and Mariners of Newcastle, otherwise known as Trinity House; incorporated by 1492 when it bought a house in Broad Chare, Newcastle, for a meeting place. Both Queen Elizabeth I and King James I granted a charter to the society under the name of the Master, Pilots and Seamen of the Trinity House of Newcastle upon Tyne. Each year the brethren elected a master, wardens and assistants to govern the fraternity and its possessions. Their jurisdiction extended to all ports and creeks between Whitby and Holy Island, and they had the sole appointment of all sea and river pilots within these limits. From 1536 they were responsible for lighthouses and pilotage in the Tyne, and not until 1865 did the Tyne Pilotage Act create a new body to examine and license fit persons as pilots, with due compensation to Trinity House for loss of revenue. Even the bishop of Durham, with all his power and influence, was barely able successfully to claim his own third of the river, and in 1554 had to cede quayside facilities in Gateshead to the mayor and corporation of Newcastle.

IMPROVEMENTS TO THE RIVER

At length, in 1850, the corporation of Newcastle lost its powers of conservancy with the River Tyne Improvement Act. Responsibility was transferred to the Tyne Improvement Commission, consisting of eighteen commissioners representing the ship-owners, coal-owners, traders, the payers of Tyne dues, and also the corporations of Newcastle, Gateshead, Tynemouth and South Shields.

The first plans for improving the Tyne included modifications to the river banks by building jetties and groynes for deepening the channel. This would be accomplished by the scouring effects of the tides. In 1861 a bill was introduced in parliament which would make the Tyne into a first-class port. The plan provided for a dredged deep-water channel as far as nineteen miles upstream. By the completion of the work, 113 million tons of sand had been dredged and dumped far out to sea. In 1852 the Tyne Improvement Commission also received parliamentary sanction to construct piers at Tynemouth and South Shields, thus forming a protective harbour at the river mouth. The north pier had a chequered career for the first fifty years of its existence. When the first stone had been laid on 15 June 1854 at Tynemouth, it was expected that it would be finished within seven years; but not until 1 April 1910 was the pier finally opened to the public. During the intervening years the wall had been breached twice by the fierce gales. In 1867, the sea was able to destroy 480ft of the 3,000ft of curved wall because of the shallow foundations. Again, in January 1897, the north pier was wrecked and the lighthouse at the end marooned for a while by a gale of forty-eight hours' duration. Finally a straight pier was designed and completed in 1909.

Not only was the Tyne straightened and deepened but several corporations including the Commissioners and the North Eastern Railway Company developed quays, docks and coal-loading staithes. Whilst the railway company built Tyne Dock at South Shields adjoining Jarrow Slake, the Commissioners constructed the Albert Edward and Northumberland Docks on the north bank. Their quay at Whitehill Point is now Tyneside's terminal port for Scandinavia, and since 1937 a regular service for passengers and cargo has existed between the quay and Bergen and Oslo. These docks and quays were all completed within fifty years of the creation of the Tyne Commission.

TYNE TRADE

Coal is still the biggest single item in the export trade of the port. The largest import on the river is iron ore. Up to a million tons are imported annually through the Tyne Dock for the Consett Iron Company. Up to 250,000 tons of grain are handled annually. The Tyne is a major importer of timber, over 200,000 tons in 1968, and the Tyne and Albert Edward Docks have been mechanised to handle cargoes of deals, battens and boards, pitwood, plywood, mahogany and hardwoods. North Shields is the most important fishing port between Hull and Aberdeen. In 1970 fish landings amounted to about 1,000,000cwt, worth £3,500,000. The industry employs 1,500 fishermen in some 500 vessels.

The Port of Tyne Authority was founded in 1968 to succeed the Tyne Commissioners and give the region conformity with its rivals of the Thames, Clyde, Mersey, Humber and Avon, each of which possess a port authority. The new Tyne authority includes not only the jurisdiction of its predecessors but also the port facilities of Newcastle upon Tyne, Gateshead and North Shields. Modern cargo handling techniques enable ships to spend a much shorter time in port; and to attract large ships the authority has decided to improve docking facilities near the river mouth at North and South Shields.

RIVER CROSSINGS

Because river-traffic makes it impracticable to have a low-level bridge, eight bridges cross the Tyne within the seven miles between Newburn and Newcastle. After Newburn bridge comes the railway bridge at Scotswood and the new road bridge there. (The latter is a steel tied arched structure of 328ft span, with a clear height of 25ft above high water.) Further downstream are the King Edward VII and High Level railway bridges.

The main road connections between Gateshead and Newcastle are the Redheugh Bridge, the High Level Bridge, the low-level Swing Bridge and the Tyne Bridge. The Redheugh is soon to be replaced. The low-level Swing Bridge is built on the site of the original Roman structure and its medieval successor. Its mechanism enables 10,000 ton coal-ships to reach the staithes at Derwenthaugh. The High Level bridge stands some 120ft above the river. Designed by Robert Stephenson and completed in 1849, it is a two-decked cast-iron structure, carrying the railway on the upper deck and the roadway beneath. The Tyne Bridge, opened by King George V in 1928, is a prominent landmark. Said to be a prototype for the Sydney Harbour bridge, it has an arch 170ft high. More than 4,000 tons of steel were used in its construction. Later, it is planned to build two more road bridges downstream.

Two ferry services exist downstream within the port authority's jurisdiction. Plying between Wallsend and Hebburn and between North and South Shields, they provide access facilities for workers in the many engineering and shipbuilding firms in the district. Under the river, between Howdon and Jarrow, are separate tunnels for pedestrians and cyclists and for motor traffic. These were built as a joint enterprise by the County Councils of Northumberland and County Durham. The intention is to provide a less congested route for traffic wishing to pass beyond Newcastle.

In subsequent chapters we shall see why all roads and sea-lanes in North East England tended to lead to Newcastle.

SELECT BIBLIOGRAPHY

N. PEVSNER and   *The Buildings of England: Northumberland* (Penguin,
I. A. RICHMOND   1957)

Chapter 2   MEDIEVAL TYNESIDE

DURING the Roman period Tyneside was part of the frontier region. About 80 AD the Roman governor of Britain, Agricola, built a fort at Benwell on his campaign northwards: and in 122 Emperor Hadrian established his stone wall westwards from Wallsend (*Segedunum*). The Roman bridge across the Tyne by the future site of Newcastle was named *Pons Aelius* in Hadrian's honour. The Anglo-Saxon period saw the foundation in 681–5 of the great monastery at Jarrow. This was the home of the Venerable Bede, 'Father of English History' (672–735).

NORMAN SETTLEMENT

Violence was the overriding factor in the history of Tyneside until the eighteenth century. The Scottish border lay within fifty miles, and in consequence Tyneside was subjected to raids and formal invasions as well as local rebellions, provoked by social discontent. William the Conqueror had founded his New Castle upon the Tyne in 1080 as much to overawe a rebellious English countryside as to check Scottish inroads into Durham and Yorkshire by the east coast route. Tynemouth had its castle by 1095.

At the time of the Norman conquest of England in 1066, the leading town on Tyneside was Newburn, a royal borough at the head of the tideway, where the river could be forded without difficulty. Copsi, earl of Northumberland, was murdered in his hall at Newburn in 1068. There is no evidence of the continued existence of any bridge downstream: the knights of William I on their way to invade Scotland in 1072, and the monks from Winchcombe travelling north in 1074 to re-establish monastic life at Jarrow, mention only ruins of a bridge. At Tynemouth, there was a parish church under the patronage of the earl of Northumberland, where a shrine had been established in 1065 to house the body of St Oswin. By 1093 this church had been transformed into a priory, dependent on the monastery of St Albans. There were also small communities at *Monkchester* and Pandon, probably represented by the subsequent parishes of St Andrew's and All Saints', Newcastle. The area was predominantly pastoral, although sufficient grain was grown to provide for immediate local needs.

From Newburn to the North Sea, the Tyne formed a boundary. The lands south of the river had been given to St Cuthbert, and for centuries the bishops of Durham continued to rule there in the tradition of Anglian landowners. Gateshead was the centre of the bishop's Tyneside authority. By 1180 Gateshead, its houses built from timber in the bishop's woods near Heworth, was a borough with meagre trading privileges. To the east lay Jarrow, still the centre of the estate donated to the monastery by its founder Ecgfrith in 681. The site had remained ruinous since its sack by the Danes about 870, any revenue being administered by the local bishop. Walcher in 1074 endowed Aldhun and his followers from Winchcombe with the Jarrow estate, and his successor as bishop, William de St Calais, obtained leave in 1083 from Pope Gregory VII to transfer these monks to Durham as his new cathedral chapter. Thereafter Jarrow became a monastic cell dependent on Durham, with about two inmates. The manors forming the estate were administered by the prior of Durham.

NEWCASTLE UPON TYNE

Because no part of Northumberland or Durham is included in the Domesday survey, we cannot measure on Tyneside the growth of population, trade or agriculture from early Norman times to the thirteenth century, when new sources of information become available. One fact, however, is outstanding. Whereas in 1080 Newcastle was a semi-derelict site, it had developed by the early twelfth century, under the shadow of its royal castle, into a substantial town with a 'head church' dedicated to St Nicholas, patron saint of merchants, sailors and children, and the dependent chapels

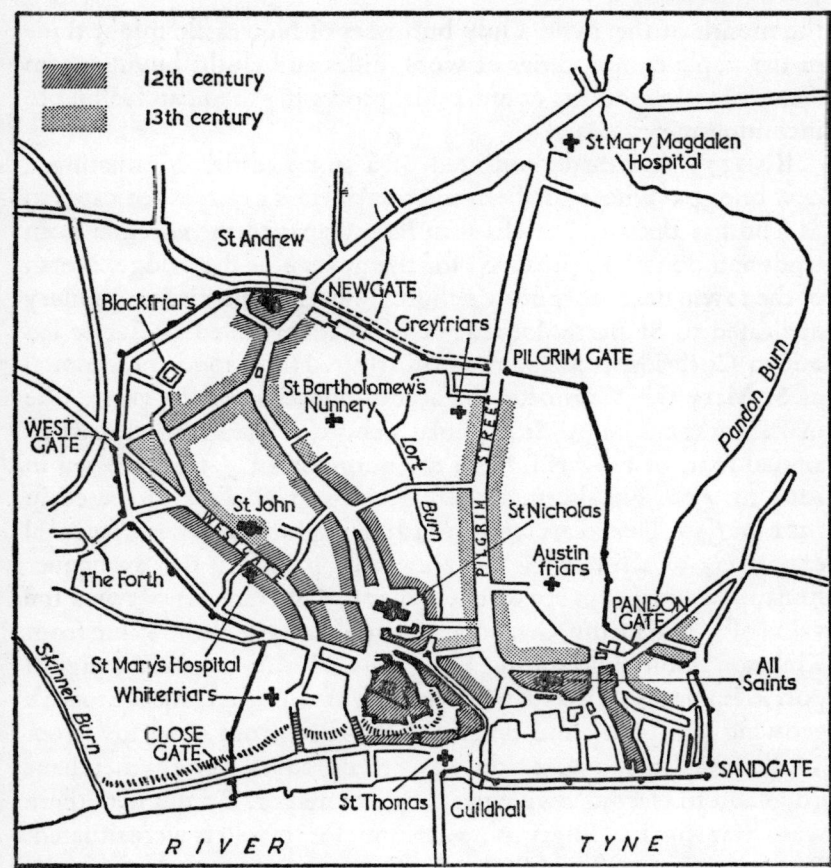

Fig 2 Medieval growth of Newcastle

of St Andrew and All Saints. Evidence of this growth is the code of burgess rights, the so-called 'Laws of Newcastle', adopted by David I for his Scottish royal boroughs after his son Prince Henry obtained possession of the town from King Stephen in 1140. From these Laws we learn that the burgesses of Newcastle were subject only to the king's reeve, entitled to hold land, buy and sell, and have law-suits settled speedily within the town. They also had special monopolistic privileges, including the right to purchase goods on board ship whilst the vessel was at anchor at the mouth of the Tyne. Only burgesses of Newcastle might trade in the staple commodities of wool, hides and cloth: buying them from the neighbouring countryside, processing them, and selling to incoming merchants.

By 1175 Newcastle consisted of a stone castle, dominating a new bridge at whose northern end was situated a chapel dedicated to St Thomas Becket. The chaplain here managed the revenue from lands and donations provided for the upkeep of the bridge. North of the town, near St Andrew's church, stood a Benedictine nunnery dedicated to St Bartholomew. A main street called Westgate led out to Corbridge, Hexham and Carlisle. Here stood the hospital of St Mary the Virgin for the accommodation of travellers. The main market adjoined St Nicholas's church. The king required an annual rent, or fee-farm, from the burgesses of £50, increased in 1201 to £60. Newburn, by comparison, paid £30, increased in 1201 to £50. Two years later, in 1203, King John imposed a national export tax of a fifteenth, and Newcastle paid into the Exchequer sums indicating exports worth £2,375. This represents twice the value of exports from Grimsby, although only half the value from Kingston upon Hull. On the same scale, Newcastle was the eighth port in England. In 1213 King John sought to profit from the town's growing prosperity and raised the fee-farm from £60 to £100. Three years later Newcastle was privileged to have a merchant guild and to elect its own chief bailiff or mayor. By this date there was a new street 'of Pilgrims', where inns for travellers were situated. In 1220 a new parish of St John's, Westgate, was carved from the existing parishes of St Nicholas's and St Andrew's.

The growth in urban population at Newcastle is underlined by the establishment there, during the thirteenth century, of the friaries of Dominicans (1261), Franciscans (1274), Carmelites (1278) and Austins (1290). By 1296 the earliest surviving Lay Subsidy roll for Northumberland reveals the presence of 275 tax-paying inhabitants in Newcastle, divided into their respective parishes. The wealthiest parish, understandably, was St Nicholas, assessed at £327 15s 4d, and its wealthiest inhabitant, Samson the cutler, was personally assessed at £53 3s 4d. The whole town was assessed at £919 2s 9½d. To this should be added the wealth and population of the industrial suburb of Pandon to the east, giving grand totals of £948 12s 5½d and 295 tax-paying inhabitants. From Pandon there was, in 1278, a complaint that fullers (cloth bleachers), dyers and brewers would be put out of business if they were prevented access to the water of Crosswell, which the Carmelite friars sought to claim for their sole use.

The best evidence about the diversity of trade in thirteenth-century Newcastle comes from the royal licence of 1265 to the corporation of the town to collect a murage or toll for the construction and maintenance of the town wall. All vendors coming to the markets at Newcastle, each Monday and Saturday, had to pay sums ranging from a farthing to three pence on goods brought for sale. The tariff mentions herring, cod and salmon in large quantities. There was wool, cloth, linen, sacking, livestock, skins and hides, fat, grain, white peas, salt, fuel including sea-coal, wine, flavourings such as almonds, garlic, onions, figs and pepper, dyestuffs such as madder and woad, with potash and alum, needed for setting the dye. There was tar, oil, oars, timber of various kinds and millstones. The absence of metals, apart from lead taxed at 2d a cartload and steel rods at ¼d a sheaf, is notable. Tyne iron-manufacture, using local deposits of ironstone, was centred to the west, at Corbridge and Bywell.

Newcastle, however, believed that its natural advantages of communication, being at once a sea-port and bridge-head, could be enhanced by suppression of all trading rivals lower down the river. The medieval bridge with its nine arches effectively barred the passage of ships upstream. In 1258 the corporation of Newcastle negotiated an agreement with the prior of Durham, who undertook not to develop the fishing community at South Shields within his manor of Westoe.

NORTH SHIELDS

The prior of Tynemouth was more obstinate. Since 1225 a fishing community had established 'shiels' or huts at the mouth of the Pow Burn, and 'North Shields' had grown until the burgesses of Newcastle in 1267 assailed its inhabitants and seized a ship moored alongside its quay. For this the burgesses were prosecuted by the abbot of St Albans, on behalf of his prior of Tynemouth, and ordered to pay £300 as damages. The prior of Tynemouth continued to encourage trading, relying on a charter of Richard I which granted the monks freedom from all tolls, with leave to have their own fishing fleet to supply their monastic house. By 1290 it was estimated that there were 100 houses at North Shields, four bakehouses and brew-houses to supply ships, and quays for mooring. This time the burgesses of Newcastle used guile rather than force. They petitioned in parliament that, because ships were now anchoring at North Shields and victualling there, the volume of trade at Newcastle was seriously diminished, which meant loss of revenue to the Crown. Edward I immediately ordered an inquiry, and in 1292 the prior of Tynemouth was ordered to dismantle the jetties at North Shields on the grounds that they were encroaching on the river. An attempt by the prior in 1304 to obtain licence for a fair at Tynemouth was successfully opposed by Newcastle.

Not until 1390 was North Shields re-established as a fishing and victualling port. Another inquiry at the instance of indignant Newcastle burgesses revealed that the prior had reclaimed four acres along the riverside, and by 1429 the settlement had increased to 200 houses, fourteen quays and thirteen bake- and brew-houses, using annually up to 1,000 quarters of wheat and 2,000 quarters of barley malt respectively. Cod and ling were being landed from boats and cobles, fishing as far away as the Shetlands and Iceland. On this occasion the Newcastle complaint fell on unsympathetic ears. In 1446 Henry VI gave the prior leave to take customs and tolls from his tenants using North Shields, a privilege later confirmed by Edward IV and including leave to export coal, salt and other wares without reference to Newcastle. In 1512, under the terms of an arbitration, the prior was again confirmed in his right to trade without paying dues at Newcastle, to have common bake-houses and breweries at North Shields and Tynemouth, and also to buy corn coming into the river in time of scarcity, although this was to be limited to a reasonable quantity.

GATESHEAD

The burgesses of Newcastle also had difficulty in restricting trade at Gateshead. This borough was controlled by the bishop of Durham, to whom it paid a fee-farm of £40 in 1180, shortly after its creation. By 1336 it claimed to have markets on Tuesday and Friday, although the burgesses of Newcastle had forcibly prevented merchants from attending these and had compelled local fishermen to bring their wares for sale in Newcastle. In 1344 the bishop of Durham was prosecuting, in his court at Durham, certain Newcastle burgesses who had made fishermen from the south bank of the Tyne sell their salmon and other fish in Newcastle, had broken the bishop's fisheries at Gateshead, Whickham, and Ryton, leased in 1338 for £13 6s 8d, and had forced boats, loaded at Whickham with coal and corn for sale downstream, to discharge at Newcastle. They had similarly prevented the loading of cargoes at Heworth, Hebburn, Jarrow and South Shields.

NEWCASTLE TRADE

The anxiety of the Newcastle burgesses to crush potential trading rivals sprang partly from the costs of success. Since the first establishment of a wooden castle in 1080—replaced in stone between 1168 and 1179—the town had grown, until by 1290 there was in addition to Westgate and Pilgrim Street a continuous line of houses and stalls from St Nicholas's church to St Andrew's, through the Iron Market, Groat Market, Bigg (or Barley) Market to the White Cross, a distance of nearly half a mile. The expanded town now required its own walls, which were started about 1265 and not completed before 1318. They consisted of a curtain wall over two miles in circumference with nineteen towers and thirty turrets, seven gateways and three posterns, and a surrounding ditch, part of which could be flooded. In addition to the costs of maintenance, the townspeople had to share in watch and ward—the duty of providing sentries and even fighting, since the Scots had started their forays in the north from 1296 onward. The other communities of Tyneside had no such military 'overheads'.

COAL

Newcastle stood repeated siege from 1315 onwards. This meant not only interruption of trade but devastation of the surrounding area, leading to the need to seek outside Tyneside for corn and other provisions. The sheep, whose wool despite its inferior quality had been the main town export, were scattered, stolen by the Scots, or killed. The cattle, whose hides had made Newcastle the chief port for leather in England until 1294, were in similar plight. At this point the Newcastle burgesses turned their attention to the exploitation of coal, which outcropped plentifully on the Town Moor, an ample area north of the town representing their common fields and pasture. There had been shipments of coal from the Tyne since the mid-thirteenth century. The ship moored at North Shields and seized by the Newcastle burgesses in 1267 had been laden with coal and hides. In 1298 the bishop of London ordered a shipload of coal to be sent from the Tyne to Gravesend. In 1351 Edward III made the significant grant to the burgesses to dig coal on the Town Moor and on the Forth, an open area to the west of the town, adjoining the manor of Elswick which belonged to the prior of Tynemouth and where by 1378 the prior had coal pits with access to coal wharves or staithes valued at £40. Coal was among the commodities that the burgesses had hindered the bishop of Durham from loading at Whickham in 1344.

By a geological quirk deep seams of coal, perhaps 1,000ft below ground elsewhere, outcropped westward in a ring from the Town Moor through Benwell to Whickham and Gateshead. This coal could be used not only for rough work such as burning limestone for mortar, or domestic heating, but also for smithy work. Extraction was simple. One dug a 'pit' into the seam, several feet below the surface, and when the coal had been removed the pit was abandoned and another started alongside. There were complaints that the roads to Newcastle were dangerous by reason of pits sunk even in the highway and left unfenced so that unwary travellers fell into them with fatal consequences.

Coal, or rather 'sea-coal' because originally it had been found on the sea-shore, washed up by the tide, was used locally to supplement timber resources. It was also used increasingly as a cargo. Economic historians long believed that Tyne coal was first exported as ballast, to keep the wooden sailing ships in balance where no other cargo was available. The burgesses of Newcastle, however, in a petition of 1363, begged that an embargo on its export be lifted because they 'have no other common merchandise in which to trade'. An analysis of one of the earliest surviving general customs rolls for Newcastle shows that, between 8 February and 29 September 1378, out of the 159 foreign ships recorded in the port all but twenty-three left with cargoes of coal. In general the incoming cargoes had been of lesser value, consisting mainly of timber, but including Swedish iron.

SHIPPING

Ships using the Tyne were small. When in 1324 Edward II had ordered that ships over forty tons should join his navy to repel a French landing, the mayor of Newcastle replied that there were only five such vessels attached to the port, ranging from 100 tons downwards. As ships grew in size, the coal-trade became increasingly dependent on the keels or lighters ferrying coal from Whickham, Gateshead and Newcastle to the ships lying downstream. In 1421 taxation of the coal-trade, a sure indication of commercial success, was levied on the keel-load, at the rate of 40 pence a keel of 20 chaldrons, originally equivalent to 360cwt. The Tyne keel was a distinctive oval-shaped craft, flat with an open hold, and propelled by two long oars, the skipper steering with one while his crew of two hauled with the other.

GUILDS

By 1515 the keelmen were included among the twenty-seven trades regulated by guilds. It was a far cry from the days when King John simply authorised the existence of 'a guild' in Newcastle. In 1342 there were twelve guilds, grouped round the basic trades of wool, leathercraft, grain, metal-working and mercery. The fifteenth century saw the addition of companies of coopers

(1436), grocers (1437), barber-surgeons and chandlers (1442), plasterers (1445), slaters (1452), and the masters and mariners of Trinity House (1492). The company of Merchant Adventurers of Newcastle was formed before 1480 by the wholesale merchants in wool, grain and mercery. They claimed the sole right to trade from Newcastle in woollen cloth, corn, grocery, silk goods, soap, tar, pitch, flax, wax, iron, wire, wainscot, clap-board, train-oil (made from whale blubber) and other Baltic produce. Their books show them sharing out lead leases among their members; and they almost certainly traded in coal and grindstones.

The growth of Newcastle and the diversification of trade is evident in the enumeration of guilds in 1515. The building trade was now represented by carpenters, masons and wallers, while increasing exports required porters, colliers, keelmen and ship-wrights. There had been reclamation from the river where it was joined by the Lort Burn before 1337, when a grant of building sites was made by Edward III on 'the Sandhill'. Also on the Sand-hill, beside the bridge-end, Roger Thornton built the Guildhall early in the fifteenth century. Further eastward of the bridge lay the Quayside, with the town wall behind, pierced by seventeen water-gates to allow maximum access with maximum security. Countless alleys lay under the shadow of the bank, crowned by All Saints' church. These led to the broader streets of Stockbridge and Cowgate, where stood the byres sheltering the town's cows, taken each morning through the gates to graze on the Town Moor. The Poll Tax returns of 1377 credited Newcastle with 2,647 tax-paying inhabitants, which made it the eleventh largest town in England after London; and this was after an outbreak of plague which was estimated to have reduced the population by a third. Another attack of plague in 1380 was estimated to have killed 6,054 inhabitants. The muster rolls of 1539 credit the town with 1,097 able-bodied men ready for its defence.

GATESHEAD

The coal-trade, which brought so much prosperity to Newcastle, also involved Gateshead. In 1384 the burgesses of Newcastle complained bitterly to Richard II that the volume of traffic at Gateshead was threatening to undermine their ability to pay taxes 'almost equal to the amount paid by York'. By the same token, the bishop of Durham as lord of Gateshead claimed that he derived a significant part of his revenue from this coal-trade. The extent of Gateshead, however, was infinitely smaller than Newcastle, and consisted of the four streets of Pipewellgate, along the river west of the bridge, Hillgate to the east of the bridge, Oakwellgate and High Street, which stretched to the top of the bank. In addition to the parish church of St Mary, there was a chapel of St Edmund and two small almshouses or hospitals. Like Newcastle, coal was worked here from outcrops in the town fields; but leave to dig was still controlled by the bishop of Durham, unlike the situation in Newcastle, where the king had transferred his rights to the burgesses. An example of such a coal lease is the grant of Bishop Thomas Hatfield on 1 April 1364 to John Plummer, burgess of Newcastle, and Walter Hesleden, burgess of Gateshead, to work coal at Gateshead for twenty-four years at an annual rent of £5. They were allowed, from the bishop's woods, timber for pit-props and for building a staithe. By 1524 the pits of neighbouring Whickham were estimated to yield 500 tons of coal a year.

SALT

At the mouth of the river at South Shields the coal-trade had married with the old fishing trade. Salt was necessary for preserving the herrings landed, and by heating brine in lead vats, later in iron tanks, using the small coal which was cheap because it was unfit for export, salt of good preservative quality was obtained. Ships lay at anchor here to receive their cargoes, brought in keels from higher up the river. In 1539 there was a brewery and nine salt-pans, and about seventy fishermen's houses. At North Shields, which had the better anchorage, the prior of Tynemouth had continued the work of reclamation making 'oon new porte and haven'. There were common bakehouses and breweries to supply the ships, as well as corn-mills, houses and salt-pans. The bulk of these buildings lay under the bank-top, described in 1565 as 'howses for fishermen . . . little kyes and shores maid before everye howse for ther cobles and there geare to ly at and to drye ther fishe and geare upon'.

Medieval Tyneside may be considered to have ended in 1530. That year the burgesses of Newcastle resolved to crush for ever the rivalry of churchmen from Durham and Tynemouth, for control of the river. The climate of opinion on the eve of the English Reformation was anti-clerical, and an act was passed in the same parliament as approved the breach with Rome. By this act 'concerning Newcastle upon Tyne and the port and haven thereunto belonging' it was forbidden to load or discharge any ship in the Tyne, saving for salt and fish, except at Newcastle. The balance of power among the Tyneside trading communities was tipped decisively in favour of Newcastle, with the weight of royal and parliamentary authority behind it.

Control of trade on the Tyne gave Newcastle a monopoly of coal-shipments in England, when shipment was the cheapest form of bulk transport.

SELECT BIBLIOGRAPHY

C. M. FRASER (ed) *Northumberland Petitions* (Surtees Soc 76, 1964)
Northumberland Lay Subsidy Roll for 1296 (Soc of Antiquaries of Newcastle, 1968)
'The Pattern of Trade in the North-East of England, 1265–1350' (*Northern History* IV, 1969)

C. M. FRASER and K. EMSLEY 'Law and society in Northumberland and Durham, 1290 to 1350' (*Archaeologia Aeliana* 4th Series XLVII, 1969)

Chapter 3   THE HOSTMEN OF
                NEWCASTLE

DURING the Middle Ages coal-mining on Tyneside had provided a vital item of trade to supply the bare necessities of life. During the succeeding centuries, it provided Tynesiders with an ample livelihood—work in the collieries themselves, their ancillary trades and the servicing industries. The managers of this complex situation were the Hostmen of Newcastle. Their name 'Hostmen' derived from the medieval practice of 'hosting', whereby a merchant strange to the town was accommodated and given necessary introductions to traders with whom he might wish to deal. They were incorporated in 1600 by Queen Elizabeth I as the company of Hostmen, authorised to have an exclusive right to trade on the Tyne in sea-coal and grindstones. Membership was drawn largely from the company of Merchant Adventurers.

The Dissolution of the Monasteries in 1539 and the confiscation of their estates had the effect on Tyneside of making coal-bearing lands available for lease from the crown. Previously such leases had been subject to strict conditions to conserve coal-resources. In 1530, when Christopher Mitford leased the mines at Elswick from the prior of Tynemouth for twenty-five years at £20 per annum, production was limited to 31 tons a day: when Henry Anderson, sometime governor of the Merchant Adventurers' Company, leased them from the crown for £68, there were no restrictions on output. On Anderson's death in January 1559 'colles wrought above the grounde at Elswicke as well at the pyttes as the staythes' were valued at £594 18s 8d. Anderson's inventory also shows him as part owner of six ships, two keels, a lighter and

29

a boat. The attraction for speculators about a crown coal-lease was that rents could be reduced if circumstances proved unfavourable, but were never increased if output exceeded expectation.

THE ATTEMPT TO ANNEX GATESHEAD

The act of 1530 had confined all shipments of coal to Newcastle quayside. In March 1553 the burgesses of Newcastle attempted another audacious coup, an act of parliament to annex Gateshead to Newcastle. In this way Gateshead coal, leased by Newcastle burgesses, could be loaded into keels on the southern bank without the need to make a token landing at the northern quay. The preamble of this act suggested that many of the artisans of Gateshead, carpenters, colliers, fishers and seamen, found employment in Newcastle; and asserted that the Tyne bridge was unfit at the Gateshead end for carts to cross. This is an extraordinary statement in view of the commercial value of the crossing, but it may have been true. Later, in 1565, the bishop of Durham as lord of Gateshead roused considerable criticism by imposing through the Durham justices of the peace a county rate for the repair of Newcastle bridge: 'being a very necessary bridge for the passage and conveyance over of her Majesty's munition and ordinance in the time of wars and for the defence of the frontier' as well as for trade and commerce. The proposed solution would have detached Gateshead from County Durham and given the Newcastle burgesses rights in Gateshead's common fields, where the coal outcropped, and in the woods of Gateshead park.

There were national implications in this act. It was sponsored by John Dudley, duke of Northumberland, whose intended prey was the bishop of Durham. The day after the annexation was approved, an act was passed to subdivide the bishopric of Durham into its component counties. The estates of the former see, estimated to be worth £2,000 a year, were annexed to the crown, and the duke hoped to secure leases on favourable terms. The new bishop of Durham would be allocated an income of £1,333 and the new bishop of Newcastle an income of £666. The death of

Edward VI, however, brought the downfall of Dudley and the quashing of the acts. Newcastle was to remain in the diocese of Durham until 1882, and Gateshead was re-united to its county. The Newcastle burgesses received compensation from the bishop of Durham in the form of a 450 years' lease of Salt Meadows, the flat southern bank of the Tyne opposite Newcastle, for use as coal-staithes.

In 1576 the Newcastle burgesses made another bid for complete control of Gateshead, when the see of Durham was vacant after the death of Bishop Pilkington. The inhabitants of Gateshead submitted a series of petitions against this revival of the act of 1553, claiming it was a borough of some 3,000 persons who were 'substantial, honest men, faithful and true subjects, as did appear in the late rebellion', and that the annexation would give Newcastle 1,000 acres of grazing and coal worth £10,000. The queen's privy council opposed the bill, the deciding factor being this question of loyalty. 'The town of Gateshead is a corporate town, an ancient borough, the key of the county palatine, the people religious, godly, and good protestants, and, besides, men of good wealth, and very civil of behaviour. The town of Newcastle are all papists . . .'

THE GRAND LEASE

The Newcastle merchants, however, had set their hearts on owning the Gateshead coal-pits. Having failed with parliament, they sought indirect means. Bishop Barnes of Durham was persuaded to lease to the queen the manors of Gateshead and Whickham to retain her favour. Subsequently, the lease was transferred by the queen to Robert Dudley, earl of Leicester, from whom it passed to Thomas Sutton, Leicester's secretary, and to the mayor and burgesses of Newcastle. The lease was to run for ninety-nine years at a rent of £90, but the true value was believed to be nearer £50,000 a year. The burgesses of Newcastle were said to have paid between £5,500 and £12,000 for the 'Grand Lease'; but administration of production was in the hands of a small group of Hostmen. This led to much discontent in Newcastle, and in

1600 the nominal lessees were authorised by the queen to transfer their interest to the mayor and burgesses of the town. It is doubtful, however, if this made any difference. Already the costs of working pits were becoming considerable.

After centuries of picking at the outcrops at Benwell, Elswick, Whickham, Gateshead, and on the Newcastle Town Moor, the topmost stratum had been exhausted. To reach greater depths required boring, which did not necessarily strike the seam at the first attempt, and might cost anything from £100 to £1,000. By the mid-sixteenth century one mine at Gateshead was 216ft deep. The deeper the mine, the more urgent the need for drainage. Pumping engines, worked by horse-, water-, or even man-power, had been introduced by the seventeenth century but could not work effectively at depths of more than 120ft. Early in the reign of Charles I, it cost the partners of Benwell colliery about £26 a week on horse-pumps to 'draw the water'. But one engine might serve more than one colliery. The pumps of Ravensworth drained every pit within a radius of three miles. In the ship–money assessment of 1636 the four principal collieries on the south bank of the Tyne at Blaydon, Stella, Ravensworth and Whickham/Gateshead were valued collectively at £9,600: and Professor Nef estimated their annual output at 200,000 tons.

This volume of coal was marketed by the Hostmen of Newcastle. Always in intention, and originally in practice, they leased the actual coal-pits. By the terms of the ancient laws of Newcastle, shippers seeking their coal-cargoes could deal only through free members of the appropriate company. The Hostmen also owned the keels which ferried the coal down to the awaiting ships. Although in 1516 keelmen had been included among the guilds of Newcastle—and presumably owned their boats—by 1638 they were largely immigrant labour from Scotland or the wild Northumbrian valleys of Tynedale and Redesdale, employed as seasonal workers by the Hostmen.

Perhaps by reason of the volume of traffic, the burgesses of Newcastle remained very sensitive to criticism of their monopoly of trade on the Tyne. In 1590 the lord mayor of London had formally complained that regulation of exports was raising the price of coal on the Thames. Although this challenge was parried by the Hostmen when in 1600 they agreed to pay the crown a new tax on exported coal—their monopoly was said to be worth £200,000 a year—the House of Commons debated the matter in 1604 and 1606. The Commons in 1621 included the Newcastle Hostmen in a list of monopolists who should have their privileges revoked; but the act of 1623 specifically exempted them.

BALLAST SHORES

Between 1614 and 1617, the corporation of Newcastle secured the creation of a conservancy commission, over which they held dominant influence, to regulate the building of staithes and the casting of ballast beside the Tyne. They also claimed sole right to lease land along the river. These pretensions were viewed with growing disquiet by local landowners who had a river frontage which could be leased as a ballast quay, a highly lucrative proposition as more and more sailing ships entered the Tyne for coal. The Newcastle corporation derived a large part of its considerable revenue from dues paid to cast ballast on its shores: they bought land for that sole purpose. Ill-stacked ballast, however, fell back into the river, reducing the depth of water for shipping.

SALT

A kindred danger to navigation on the river was that refuse from the salt-pans at North and South Shields could fall or be thrown into the river, or that ships coming for salt, a manufacture similarly protected by a monopoly granted to the Society of Salt-makers in 1634, might cast ballast at the mouth of the Tyne. Between 1632 and 1635, the earl of Northumberland began systematically to buy up existing salt-pans on his land at North Shields and to extend operations until by 1638 there were thirty such 'pans' at work to the east and west of the town. At Howdon and at South Shields, the dean and chapter of Durham were encouraging a similar expansion of the salt trade. It required 50cwt of coal to produce a ton of salt; and in this way coals which the

C

Hostmen prevented from being sold at Newcastle could still bring the owners a profit in industry. By 1667 there were 121 salt-pans at South Shields. Further pans were established on the coast at Cullercoats, using coal dug at Whitley. Travellers claimed to be able to see the smoke and steam from sixteen miles away.

GLASS

A growing timber shortage in England had led to legislation in 1615 forbidding the use of wood as fuel in glass-works. Previously glass had been fused in small clay crucibles, the heat being applied by banking the pots in wood, the 'potash' falling periodically inside the crucible, helping with the chemical reaction. At the same time as the prohibition, a patent was issued to the company of Sir Edward Zouche to manufacture 'all manner of drinking glasses broad glass window glass looking glasses and all other kinds of glasses bugles bottles vials or vessels . . . with sea coal, pit coal or any other fuel whatsoever not being timber or wood'. Shortly afterwards Sir Robert Mansell, sometime admiral of the Narrow Seas fleet, joined the company and soon had bought out all his partners. Actual production was in the hands of French Huguenot immigrant workers. Tyneside with its ample coal resources and good sea communications was an obvious centre for manufacture and the first recorded appearance in Newcastle of the Lorrainer families of Hennezel, Thisac, Thiétry and Houx was in 1619. Their specialities were window-glass and tall, narrow beakers and bottles.

The Tyneside glassworks were sited on the east bank of the Ouseburn, near its mouth. Here they had a ready supply of coal and easy access to the Tyne. Distribution was done by way of the London collier fleet, crates of glass being packed among the coal to prevent movements in the ship's hold and consequent breakages. Lacking the natural re-agent of wood ash the glass mixture was difficult to control. The crucibles now required lids to prevent soot and coal-ash falling into the 'melt', and this in turn made a greater heat necessary. Mansell's glass had a poor reputation as 'scarce, bad and brittle . . . a sort of ash colour'. By September

1640 Mansell's three glass-houses at Byker, valued by him at £4,000, were producing 3,000 cases of glass a year, each case worth 25s. At the outbreak of the Civil War Tyneside was the principal centre in England for window-glass; and the presence to this day on Sandhill of seventeenth-century merchants' houses with glass frontages on four storeys testifies to Newcastle's pride in its local product.

EAST ANGLIAN COLLIERS

The coal trade and its subsidiaries of salt and glass dominated Tyneside. Ships came to the river for all three commodities, leaving their ballast as a memento of the journey. But the coal-owning Hostmen's control stopped short of these ships, which were owned largely by East Anglian or London merchants. It was in the interest of these latter to keep down the shipment price of coal, to profit by the difference when it was retailed in the south. In 1622 the issue became crucial, when the ship-owners joined with London merchants to allege an attempt by the Hostmen to sell good coal mixed with slate or pan-coal to compensate for overproduction from poor seams. The Hostmen amended their ways; but in 1637 they stopped giving the shippers overmeasure at the rate of one ton free in every five sold. At the same time they bargained with Charles I for the right to regulate the quantity of coal each colliery should produce. In return the Hostmen agreed to pay the king an extra shilling on every Newcastle chaldron shipped from the Tyne. The East Anglian ship owners promptly refused to sail to Newcastle for coal, on the grounds that loss of over-measure and higher prices at the staithes would deprive them of their reasonable profits. Their boycott compelled the crown to reconsider its grant of monopoly to the Hostmen.

CIVIL WAR

The question of the London fuel supply was of national concern. By 1636 Charles I had alienated his support among landowners by the imposition of ship-money. His introduction of a Prayer Book into Scotland had roused the Scottish Presbyterian Church and in 1639 brought a Scottish army into Northumberland. To find the money to induce the Scots to withdraw, Charles needed to assemble a parliament to grant taxation. He also required support in the country. The Newcastle Hostmen offered a certain revenue from coal-shipments in return for recognition of their coal monopoly. At this stage, in August 1640, the Scots again advanced into England and captured Newcastle, after routing royalist forces under Lord Conway and Sir Jacob Astley at Newburn. The Tyne coal trade was now in the hands of the Scots, who had the chance of selling coal to recover their costs of quartering. In fact, the Scots agreed to withdraw on receipt of a levy of £850 a day for two months and on the understanding that they retained as surety Newcastle, Durham and the coastal towns north of the Tees, except Berwick. Trade in the mines and glass-works was disrupted and shipping avoided the river for fear of commandeering.

Newcastle corporation paid £38,888 to the Scots. As Dr Pocklington wrote drily to Sir John Lambe in 1640 on the capture of the town: 'This mischief might have been prevented if the town and adjacent countries would have supplied Sir Jacob Astley with £3,000 to draw up an army for their defence, but they answered they could not possibly levy so great a sum; and now these very men have compounded with Lesley [the Scottish commander] to pay his army about £12,000 every month'. The inhabitants, from the magistrates down to the humblest trader or workman, once more looked on the Scots as the traditional enemy. There was no demur when on 20 June 1642 the king appointed Lord William Cavendish as governor of Newcastle and the four northern counties. Gun emplacements were erected at North and South Shields to control shipping at the mouth of the Tyne.

Parliament took alarm. It already had abolished the duties payable on Tyne coal, lest it form a source of royal revenue outside its control. Following the outbreak of Civil War, the Lords and Commons passed on 14 January 1643 an ordinance forbidding ships to sail to Newcastle for coal or salt or to carry corn there 'until that town of Newcastle shall be freed of and from the forces there now raised or maintained against the Parliament'. This blockade of the Tyne was designed to prevent the king profiting from sale of coal to Holland, the source of his armaments. The Hostmen had no collier fleet at their disposal, nor had the king a navy to protect ships running the blockade. The Scots had promised to supply London with coal from Fife. They also sent an army under General Lesley, now earl of Leven, to drive the royalist troops out of Tyneside. The Scots took up their positions outside Newcastle on 3 February 1644. The royalist governor, now marquis of Newcastle, had rejoined his garrison the day before. Heavy siege artillery was landed at Blyth on 6 February; but with the garrison reinforced, the Scots withdrew by way of Newburn and crossed south into County Durham and Yorkshire. On the way, they mounted a successful assault on the fort at South Shields.

Scottish pressure being reduced, the marquis of Newcastle withdrew some of his forces to strengthen the royalist army in Yorkshire, and was involved in the disaster of Marston Moor. Meanwhile a second Scottish army under the earl of Callander had marched into Northumberland and on 15 August the sieges of Newcastle and Tynemouth re-commenced. The walls of Newcastle were still in good order, and after suitable embanking, guns were mounted upon them. The city fathers, seriously impoverished by the blockade of the town, urged a spirited resistance to their trade enemies. Systematic bombardment and the springing of mines eventually breached the walls and the western half of the town fell to the Scots on 19 October. The royalist leaders retreated into the old keep, where they maintained themselves for a further two days, but finding that Lesley would give them no safe-conduct, they surrendered on 21 October. Tynemouth fell on 27 October, the garrison's will to resist being undermined by the plague.

The surrender of Newcastle and Tynemouth to the Scots was viewed by the English parliament with mixed feelings, for the Scots now had control of the Tyne coal trade and did not finally agree to evacuate Tyneside until 30 January 1647. In December

1647, Sir Arthur Hesilrige was nominated by parliament as the new governor of Newcastle and Tynemouth, and given two regiments of foot as garrison; and in April 1648 parliament allocated £5,000 for repair of their fortifications. Meanwhile, the royalists played on the sentiments of Lieutenant-Colonel Henry Lilburn, Heselrige's deputy at Tynemouth. In August 1648 Lilburn declared for Charles I, released the prisoners in the castle and threatened to pistol any in his garrison 'that would not be for himself and King Charles'. He opened the gates for recruits to the royalist cause among the seamen at North Shields. Heselrige promptly sent a force down the river and recaptured the castle. So ended the fighting on Tyneside: and a pamphleteer summarised the situation as follows: 'Let this gallantry of Sir Arthur Heselrige and the stormers never be forgotten. Let London especially remember this, for unlesse so happily regained, no more coles could be expected this year'.

Now that parliament had control of Tyneside it might be thought that the stranglehold of the Newcastle Hostmen over the coal trade would be ended, more especially as many of the most important Newcastle coal-owners were manifest royalists. These had their estates sequestered, and pending redemption their collieries were available for lease by persons well-affected to parliament. Men, however, such as Sir Lionel Maddison and John Blakeston, who could be regarded as Puritans, still traded according to the regulations of the Hostmen's Company. By 1645 the Company was fining members again for loading coals at Shields and for 'clearing' the coals of non-Hostmen colliery owners. The corporation, now purified of royalists, was similarly zealous for the liberties of members of its guilds.

RALPH GARDINER

Undeterred, the men of North and South Shields persevered with their salt-making, trimming of ballast-shores, loading of coals and victualling of ships. They also offered to repair ships damaged on entry into harbour. Such services infringed the monopolies not only of the Hostmen but also of the companies of Bakers and Brewers and of Shipwrights. In the forefront of the struggle was Ralph Gardiner, brewer, and, since about 1646, the lessee of coal pits at Flatworth. In 1650 his colliery lease was sequestrated on the grounds that his predecessor had been a royalist. Shortly afterwards, the Newcastle company of Brewers proceeded against him for supplying ships at Shields from his brewery there. In 1652 Gardiner was imprisoned in Newcastle for continuing to brew. He was back in prison by September 1653, when he petitioned parliament to investigate the restrictions imposed by the Newcastle companies on Tyne trade. The Council of Trade considered the matter, referring it to a hearing by parliament on 13 December 1653. The previous day, however, parliament was dissolved and Gardiner was left to castigate Newcastle in his book *England's Grievance Discovered*. Here he argued that the corporation, blind with greed, was allowing the Tyne to silt up to preserve its profits from ill-kept ballast shores, preventing free sale of coals in order to monopolise the profits, and callously jeopardising men's lives to maintain its market and guild privileges.

Gardiner's complaints paint a lively picture of conditions on the river: 'the great fleets of ships daily riding' at North Shields; in winter, the Tyne frozen over, with the consequent difficulty of getting to Newcastle as it was easier to reach by boat than by road, since the highways were lined with coal pits into which, when they were covered with snow, it was easy for man and beast to tumble. As market regulations prevented traders from selling at North Shields, prices at Newcastle were artificially inflated so that 'the poor could not buy [corn], but have been constrained to eat beasts' blood baked, instead of bread . . . many country people were necessitated to eat dogs and cats, and to kill their poor little coal-horses for food . . . many have been found starved to death in holes.' The same facts, without the prejudice, are recognised by William Gray in his *Chorographia*, the earliest history of Newcastle, written in 1649. Here he tells how all Tyneside repaired to the markets at Newcastle on a Saturday, to buy meat and poultry:

> . . . the reason is not the populousness of the Town that makes it, it is the people in the Country (within ten miles of the Town) who makes their

provision there, as likewise all that lives by Coale-trade, for working and conveying Coales to the water; as also the shipping which comes into this River for Coales, there being sometimes three hundred sayles of ships.

Gardiner's accusations at London were stoutly repudiated by Newcastle's representatives, who denied illegality in their enforcement of ancient privilege. By July 1659, however, the Hostmen recognised that some compromise must be reached with the 'unfree' coal-owners as regards shipping their coal and even loading at North Shields. They were saved from this capitulation by the restoration of Charles II in May 1660. For the remainder of the seventeenth century, the Hostmen enforced their monopoly of the coal trade, seizing coal offered by unfree merchants, fining members who marketed coals for unfree men, and seeking to impose restriction on shipments of coal from Cullercoats or Sunderland. They tried to demolish the wharves and quayside houses at North Shields, and in 1672 succeeded in suppressing the brewery of John Overing there.

Nevertheless, the tide in favour of the Hostmen had already begun to ebb. The volume of trade was such that a specialisation of enterprise was desirable. Coal-owners concentrated on technical improvements in the working of the collieries or in methods of delivery at the staithes, leaving to Newcastle 'free' coal merchants only the actual sale of coal to ship-owners. The Hostmen could still effectively control the coal trade by regulating the volume of sales and by owning the keels which brought the coal down river. Soon, however, the colliery owners would make their own arrangements and tie the services of the Hostman to a particular colliery. He would then be simply an agent.

TYNESIDE POPULATION

A picture of Tyneside shortly after the Restoration can be derived from the Hearth Tax returns of 1663-5. This tax was imposed on all householders having three or more chimneys. On the national scale, Newcastle stood as the fourth most populous provincial town in England, after Norwich, York and Bristol. The actual householders named, both exempt and non-exempt, numbered 2,510. The most populous ward within the town was Sandgate, the keelmen's and sailors' quarter, with 644 houses, of which no less than 510 were exempt from tax because of their small size. The wealthiest of the twenty-four wards was that associated with the Pink Tower, although the houses were actually situated in the Close and the Sandhill. Here there were no exempt householders and the thirty houses averaged seven taxable chimneys each. Across the river at Gateshead were to be found 633 householders. Here large houses stood amid small workmen's cottages. One of the more notable inhabitants, Robert Trollopp, 'gentleman', had been architect of the Newcastle Guildhall when it was rebuilt at a cost of £9,774 after the bombardment of 1644. Trollopp was concerned that Gateshead should evolve some guild organisation to oppose the pretentions of the Newcastle companies, and is believed to have been instrumental in persuading Bishop Cosin in 1671 to incorporate the 'portmanteau' guild of freemasons, carvers, stonecutters, sculptors, brickmakers, tilers, bricklayers, glaziers, paint stainers, founders, nailers, pewterers, plumbers, millwrights, saddlers, bridlers, trunkmakers and distillers.

The Hearth Tax returns enable some estimate to be made of the size of the communities scattered along the banks of the Tyne in 1663–5. After Newcastle and Gateshead, the most populous place was South Shields, with an estimated 567 householders. The total of householders on Tyneside was about 5,000. On surviving map evidence the individual communities tended to straggle either along the bankside, with the widespread use of boat-transport, or along the roads serving the pits. In some places, such as Gibside or Axwell, the form of the hearth tax returns suggests that the pitmen lived in isolated cottages—not even straggling hamlets.

It was a bustling area, with glassworks and salt-pans downstream from Newcastle and by 1691 a nascent iron industry at Winlaton; but all was dependent on coal, its extraction and distribution. There were pitmen, keelmen and seamen on the one hand, and owners of collieries and ships on the other:

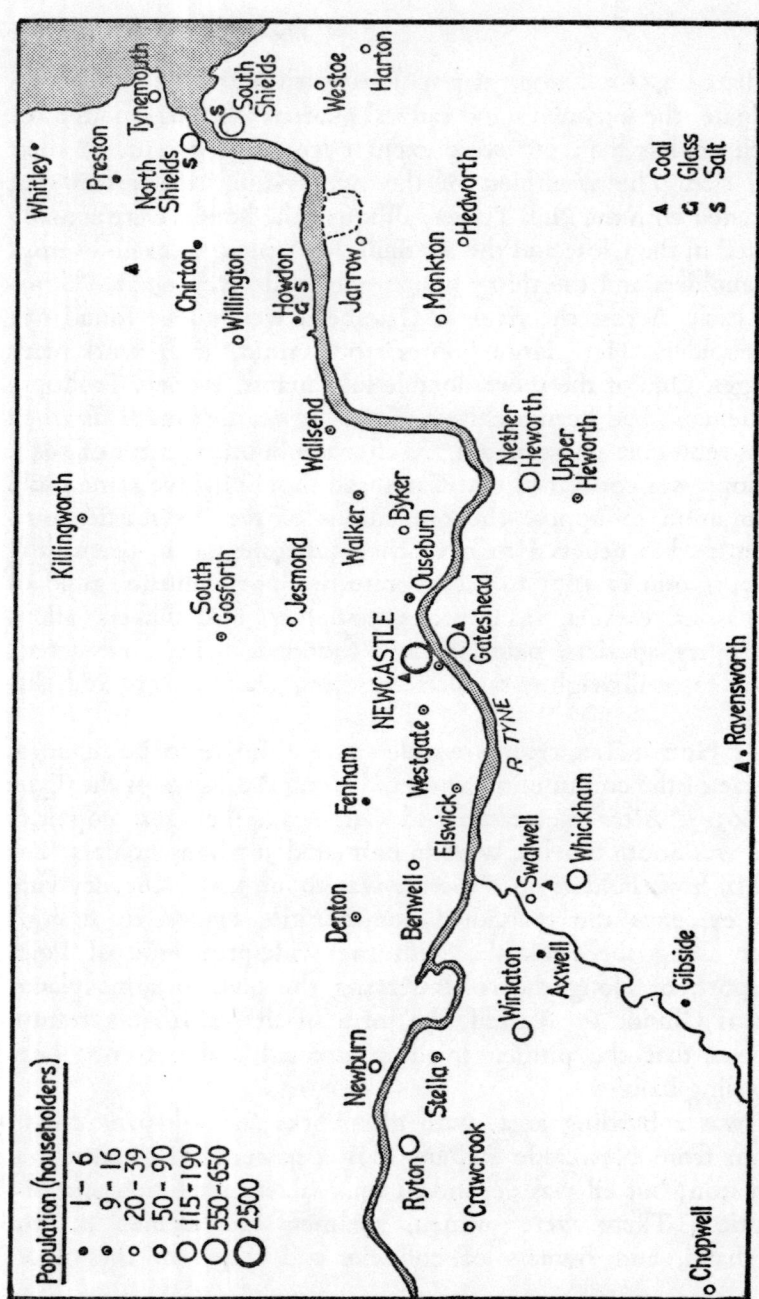

Fig 3 Tyneside about 1665

Population (householders)
• 1 – 6
•• 9 – 16
○ 20 – 39
○ 50 – 90
○ 115 – 190
○ 550 – 650
○ 2500

▲ Coal
G Glass
s Salt

and still organising the distribution were the Hostmen of Newcastle.

SELECT BIBLIOGRAPHY

F. W. DENDY (ed)	*The Newcastle Hostmen's Company* (Surtees Soc 105, 1901)
R. GARDINER	*England's Grievance Discovered* (1665, reprinted 1796)
W. GRAY	*Chorographia* (1649: reprinted in various editions)

Chapter 4   LOCAL GOVERNMENT ON
TYNESIDE TO 1835

REMOTE ORIGINS
            UNTIL recently, local government in England
and Wales was based on units originating in Anglo-Saxon times.
These units were the shire, the parish, and an intermediate area
known variously as the hundred, wapentake, or (in Northumberland and Durham) the ward. In these terms, Tyneside north of
the river lay in Northumberland, within the ward 'between
Tyne and Wansbeck' or Castle Ward, whilst Tyneside south of
the river lay in County Durham, within the Chester [le Street]
Ward. For ordinary judicial purposes there were the shire courts
of Northumberland and Durham, the latter being controlled by the
bishop of Durham as count palatine. The Norman Conquest super-
imposed on the area a system of baronial and manorial courts.
   For many purposes, including rate assessment, the basic unit
was the parish. The origin of three of these on Tyneside can be
traced to monastic estates, namely Jarrow, founded by King
Ecgfrith in 681 and extending across the Tyne to Wallsend;
Gateshead, mentioned incidentally by the Venerable Bede in 651,
and Tynemouth, whose first monastery was destroyed by the
Danes about 800. Two Newcastle parishes may have pre-Norman
antecedents. Early tombstone fragments have been found near St
Andrew's—possibly the church of *Monkchester*; and Pandon, with
its church of All Saints, has been claimed as the site of Bede's *Ad
Murum*; Newburn represents the New Borough of the Nor-
thumbrian earls at the head of the tideway; and Ryton, an estate
of the bishop of Durham, is notable as being the only part of
County Durham north of the River Derwent. Ryton, indeed,

44

provides a fine example of county boundaries being influenced by considerations of land ownership. With the introduction after 1361 of justices of the peace, administrative business concerning Tyneside was conducted on a county level, although after 1400 Newcastle had not only its borough court but also its own bench of magistrates.

The Norman Conquest was slow to take effect on Tyneside. Until the rebellion of Earl Waltheof in 1074, William I left northern government in local hands. Thereafter he appointed Walcher, bishop of Durham, as the new earl of Northumberland. Bishop Walcher, who came from Lorraine, ruled his earldom on the advice of an English council in order to preserve the old administrative forms. In May 1080 Walcher summoned a folk-moot at Gateshead to consider grievances brought against his Norman knights. Attending in person, Walcher was attacked by an angry mob and murdered. This outrage immediately provoked the Conqueror to ravage Tyneside in reprisal and to plant a 'New Castle' opposite the offending ancient centre at Gateshead. At the same time measures were taken to encourage a trading community at the castle gates, with a new church dedicated to St Nicholas, patron of merchants.

BOROUGH FEE-FARMS

This community grew, as is evidenced by Henry II's confirmation of the Laws of Newcastle, as enjoyed by the burgesses in the time of his grandfather, Henry I. Subsequent references to Newcastle during the twelfth century confirm that it was controlled by a royal bailiff with judicial authority; although, by 1170, the town had won partial financial independence through payment of an annual farm or rent of £50 to the royal exchequer. A similar arrangement existed at Newburn, where the annual farm to the Crown was £30. At Gateshead the immediate lord was the bishop of Durham: and here the borough bailiff was appointed by the bishop until 1620, after which date the Select Vestry of Gateshead assumed authority for local administration.

Most of Tyneside in the Middle Ages was agricultural. The

villagers performed typical labour services on the lord's demesnes at Tynemouth, Westoe and Whickham, and their succession to land and the settlement of complaints were dealt with at the respective halmote courts of the prior of Tynemouth, the prior of Durham and the bishop of Durham. The borough of Newburn passes from view after 1205, when it was granted to the lord of Warkworth by King John in recognition of his past services. The rental known as Bishop Hatfield's Survey, made before 1381, shows that the borough of Gateshead was then leased for £22.

NEWCASTLE CORPORATION

The sole growth point on Tyneside for popular local government was at Newcastle. In 1213 King John, when raising the town farm to £100, promised freedom from interference in its affairs by the sheriff of Northumberland or by the constable of the royal castle of Newcastle. Three years later, in 1216, the town elected Daniel, son of Nicholas, as its chief bailiff, and by 1223 there was a 'common seal of the corporation of Newcastle' bearing the punning device of a castle. In 1251 royal approval was given that the chief bailiff be styled 'mayor', and that coroners be appointed for the town, thus separating Newcastle from the jurisdiction of the county coroners in matters of sudden death, treasure-trove, claiming of sanctuary by felons, and the like. No indication is given of the method of selection of these municipal officers.

The first regulation of election procedure arose from a violent contest in 1341 between the supporters of John Denton, who had already served in that office in 1333, 1336 and 1340, and those of Richard Acton, mayor in 1334. Denton claimed that he was the choice of the 'wiser and better burgesses', but Acton's supporters seized the town gates and royal intervention was necessary to preserve the town from Scottish attack. The immediate occasion for this action was a municipal scandal: that John Denton had fraudulently acquired from the king land in the Sandhill properly belonging to the town, had misappropriated funds for the repair of the town bridge and walls, and used the processes of justice to harass his rivals. The opportunity, however, was taken to voice two deeper-seated town grievances. One was for equality of trade for rich and poor burgesses alike; and the other was for the control of town administration by all the guilds. King John in 1216 had permitted the formation of a town guild. As no trade was specified, presumably it was permission for a general regulation of standards and apprenticeships. (Berwick-upon-Tweed never developed differentiated companies and its corporation was controlled by 'the Guild'.)

Between 1308 and 1342 the rich, wholesale merchants had formed themselves into the companies of woollen merchants, boothmen or corn merchants, and mercers—who re-amalgamated before 1480 to form the Merchant Adventurers' Company—whilst the lesser tradesmen associated themselves into the remaining nine guilds of bakers, skinners, saddlers, tanners, cordwainers, butchers, smiths, fullers and tailors. The new election procedure of 1342 declared that future mayors would be chosen by a committee of twenty-four, consisting of two representatives from each of the town guilds. Other clauses of the charter reaffirmed the trading privileges of all burgesses and required publicity for the corporation's finances and care in the management of corporation property. These provisions were designed to counterbalance the power of the wholesale merchants, and it is significant that as soon as conditions stabilised in Newcastle the charter of confirmation by Edward III, dated 20 October 1342, was officially repudiated. From 24 October 1345, the mayor of Newcastle was to be selected by a committee composed of the previous mayor and bailiffs of the town.

The duties of the mayor and the four bailiffs before 1400 can only be inferred. They certainly attended the borough court, which heard pleas brought by burgesses or to which they were parties. The borough court was also used for registration of title deeds. Any wife with property had to give her personal consent 'within the four benches' of the borough court before this could be disposed of by her husband, and the names of the town bailiffs are known mainly from their regular appearance as witnesses in title deeds.

The next milestone in the development of Newcastle's government was its detachment from the county of Northumberland on 23 May 1400 and creation as a county in itself by Henry IV, in return for support of his overthrowal of Richard II. Henceforth a sheriff would be elected annually by the committee of twenty-four burgesses responsible for the selection of the mayor. The sheriff came by subsequent custom to preside as judge over the court responsible for hearing all pleas, brought in the Guildhall, by burgesses touching their lands or trading disputes, where one party was *not* a freeman of Newcastle. Where both parties were freemen, the case was brought before the mayor's court. By the early nineteenth century, both these courts were weekly. Also conferred in 1400 was the right to elect six aldermen, who, with the mayor, would be justices of the king's peace within the town to enforce the Statute of Labourers and Artificers. They were not competent, however, to judge felonies in general without special royal authority. The four bailiffs who had previously acted with the mayor were forthwith superseded.

Little is known of the municipal government of Newcastle during the fifteenth century. The number of trade guilds steadily increased, and by 1515 there were twenty-one bye-trades in addition to the original twelve 'mysteries'. Roughly grouped according to occupation, these were the colliers, keelmen, porters and shipwrights; the daubers, slaters, tilers, masons and wallers; the weavers, girdlers and shalloon weavers; the millers and cooks; the spurriers, furbishers, bowyers and arrowsmiths; the coopers, the wrights and the barbers. Membership of these lesser guilds brought with it merely the freedom to exercise a particular craft, and no general licence to trade in the town or to participate in government, apart from attendance at the 'guild day' thrice a year at St Nicholas's church, when apprenticeships were formally registered and guild freedoms proclaimed. By tradition on these occasions, common grievances might be ventilated by the freemen, although the corporation was not bound to remedy them.

The royal court of Star Chamber decreed on 2 May 1516 that general trading was limited to members of the guilds of mercers,

drapers, corn-merchants and spicers, although lesser freemen could
be admitted to these guilds on payment of an appropriate entrance
fee. The battle for free trading by freemen who were not of the
Merchant Adventurers' Company was not won until 1730, when
the merchants prosecuted George Dixon, a freeman-baker, for
buying corn; but their bill in the court of Exchequer was dismissed
with costs. Thereafter there was no legal protection for Newcastle wholesale merchants against freemen who exercised a right
given them by the twelfth-century Laws of Newcastle and re-
confirmed in 1342, 1371, 1378 and 1438–9.

TOWN OLIGARCHY UNDER THE TUDORS AND STUARTS

The evolution of a common council may be traced from 1557,
when a charter of Philip and Mary increased the number of elected
aldermen from six to ten and established that the twenty-four
electors should be assistants to the mayor and aldermen for the
following year and 'taken of the common council'. It also stipulated
that the electoral body for the mayoralty should include four
aldermen. The earl of Rutland, president of the Council of the
North, ratified these provisions in August 1561, with the limita-
tion that twelve of the electing body must be either aldermen or
former mayors and sheriffs. This ensured complete control of
municipal affairs by the establishment: in fact, by the company
of Merchant Adventurers and later by the Hostmen. By a charter
of August 1589, Newcastle was granted an Admiralty court, with
jurisdiction over offences committed on board ship or in the river
between Spar Hawk and Hedwin Streams. The mayor and corporation were also empowered to hold courts of gaol delivery and
erect a gallows, a jurisdiction over criminal matters which had
been reserved to the Crown in the charter of 1400. A charter of
1600 constituted the mayor, recorder and aldermen as justices of
the peace and of gaol delivery. Finally a decree of the Council of
the North, confirmed by James I on 31 March 1604, modified the
composition of the selection committee for the mayoralty by
giving representation to the fifteen bye-trades in addition to the

twelve ancient companies. (There remained nine companies still unrepresented.) This charter of 1604 also notes that the Common Council consisted of 'twenty-four others', whose method of selection is not specified.

In theory the common council was a counterweight to the mayor and aldermen and chosen at the discretion of the guilds. In fact, as the 'reformers' bitterly alleged, it was packed with friends and relations of the mayor and aldermen. This was the more serious in that the council was responsible for approving leases of town land, including the ballast shores. Other grievances were corporation connivance at trading within the town by non-freemen, and appropriation by the mayor of money paid for town offices, including that of town clerk. These charges were presented to Charles I by a delegation of four burgesses in June 1633, together with the allegation that the mayor and aldermen were stifling the political significance of the traditional guild day by attending late (at ten in the morning) and leaving early, as soon as grievances were aired, so bringing business to a close.

Unrest in Newcastle over the oligarchic character of its municipal government is unusual, however, in that the vocal reformers simply wanted to join the ruling caste and made no pretence that the privileges should be opened to a wider group of inhabitants.

Following the capture of Newcastle by the Scots in October 1644, Royalist sympathisers were purged from the corporation and eight new faces joined the common council. Two, however, were already Hostmen and three quickly took up membership of that company. The old allegations continued to be heard that voting procedure in elections were irregular, and John Cosins, a Puritan of long standing, was expelled from the aldermanic bench in 1647 for denying the legality of the then mayor, aldermen and common council. Cosins sued unsuccessfully for his restoration to the bench, and the strength of feeling in the town was indicated by an attack on the person of the new mayor, Thomas Bonner, in 1648, when a small but angry mob also stoned Bonner's house. Town office still depended on connections.

At the Restoration the Puritan faction was eliminated, although other aldermen having no Royalist traditions continued in office because they had the right connections. Now, however, royal interference became of great significance, and in 1684 Newcastle's charters were revoked, in common with most boroughs, and a new charter issued which reserved to the Crown power to displace the mayor and aldermen.

Renewed action against the corporation was taken by James II, who by a mandate of 15 December 1685 ordered the replacement of the existing common council by one of a broader religious complexion. This was followed in December 1687 by the royal rejection of the mayor (John Squire), six aldermen, the sheriff (William Ramsay Jr), the deputy recorder and fifteen of the common council. The electors were instructed to choose named Catholics. Some beneficiaries, however, of the royal intervention were Dissenters, including Ambrose Barnes, who had been an alderman during the Commonwealth. While all was in confusion—'Men were at a loss to see how suddenly the world was changed, the cap, the mace, and the sword, one day carried to the church, another day to the mass-house, another day to the dissenting-meeting-house'—yet another charter was given to Newcastle, restricting the election of the corporation and of members of parliament to the existing mayor and aldermen. This would have brought town administration wholly under royal control.

Despite pressure the guild electors at Michaelmas 1688 refused to approve the royal nominations for mayor and sheriff. Legal opinion was sought and it was stated that the new charters were void. Thus fortified, new elections of Protestant officers were held; and the accession of William of Orange and Queen Mary was accepted without demur.

OLIGARCHY UNDER THE HANOVERIANS

Thereafter borough affairs came to rest in the hands of prominent merchant families such as the Blacketts and the Ridleys, whose diversified interests ranged from coal and lead leases and land ownership to banking and industrial enterprises, such as glassworks. Restrictive trading by guildsmen had been effectively

abolished by 1730, but the medieval constitution of the corporation still gave considerable political power to the freemen of
Newcastle. The mayor controlled the local militia and, in times
of unrest due to rising prices or the activities of the press-gang,
could call upon the military to fire upon rioters. The worst such
crisis occurred in 1740, after an exceptionally severe winter when
the Tyne froze over, preventing its use by shipping. Bread-grain
rose to an exorbitant price, and on 9 June a mob of pitmen,
keelmen and sailors clamoured for action to set a just price. The
militia was called out, but an announcement was made simul-
taneously that the aldermen would fix prices on the following
day. No further action seems to have been taken for nearly a
fortnight, when rumour spread that ships loaded with grain were
leaving the Tyne to supply markets where there was still greater
scarcity. Many of the corn shops put up their shutters and refused
to sell at the regulated prices. All this time the militia was standing
in readiness to act in case of riots. On 25 June the mayor, Cuthbert
Fenwick, disbanded the militia, largely composed of merchants'
apprentices; and the hungry populace marched on the Guildhall
to urge further action by the mayor against the corn merchants.
While the militia was being hastily re-assembled the rioters broke
into the Guildhall, ransacked the mayor's parlour, rifled the town
treasury of an estimated £1,200, and destroyed corporation
archives. After this they ranged the streets in search of food shops.
Meanwhile, by the evening of 26 June, three companies of regular
soldiers from Alnwick entered Newcastle and rounded up the
rioters, forty of whom were arrested. Seven of these were subsequently convicted of riot and sentenced to transportation for
seven years.

The corporation might control the working population by
force, but it should not be regarded as a wholly reactionary body.
In 1763 it promoted a private act of parliament to provide street
lighting and a night patrol, the expenses to be defrayed on behalf
of the corporation from a parish rate. Again, in 1786, it obtained
powers to organise collection of refuse, to regulate traffic conges-
tion where goods were loaded and unloaded, to restrict the areas

which might be used for display of goods for sale to the recognised public markets, and to widen streets and build new ones—using compulsory purchasing powers if necessary.

Nevertheless, some freemen resented the assumption that members of the corporation alone had regard for the welfare of Newcastle. They, too, sought to work through parliament, but to restrict the powers of the corporation to regulate navigation on the Tyne. This was probably the most vulnerable chink in the corporation's armour, because revenue from river dues was the major source of its income but a minor field of expenditure. The plan of campaign for those wishing to improve Tyne navigation was to use their parliamentary franchise (restricted to freemen of Newcastle) to elect representatives at Westminster who would be sympathetic to their aims.

The cost of a contested parliamentary election was prohibitive, and it is a measure of local feeling that after thirty-three years of returning local merchants there should be three contests within six years, namely in 1774, 1777 and 1780. The sitting member in 1774 was Sir Walter Calverley Blackett, his fellow member of previous years having resigned. Blackett had represented Newcastle in parliament since 1734, been mayor of the town on five occasions, and for his charities had earned the titles of the Patriot, Father of the Poor and King of Newcastle. By 1774 he was sixty-seven years of age and had recently incurred unpopularity by supporting the pretension of the common council of Newcastle to lease the Nuns' Moor, a tract of pasture adjoining the Town Moor. In December 1771 about 87 acres were advertised to be let, and a Mr Hopper took up this lease and enclosed the land for growing corn. Some of the freemen regarded the action of the common council as an infringement of their privileges, which included the right to graze two cows on the Moor; and on legal advice they broke down Hopper's hedge and depastured his corn with their cattle. Hopper sued the freemen and the common council sought leave to regulate the matter by private act of parliament. This act authorised resident freemen and resident widows of deceased freemen to graze two cows each on the

Moor, but permitted the enclosure of up to 100 acres at any one period, the rents to be applied to the use of poor freemen and their widows.

The combination of encroachment on their pasturage privileges and lack of concern over the state of the River Tyne, whose conservancy was the acknowledged responsibility of Newcastle corporation, fired a group of freemen, local merchants and shippers to introduce as possible parliamentary candidates the Hon Constantine Phipps, a naval captain and polar explorer, and Thomas Delaval, merchant, engineer and inventor. The hope was that enough freemen would 'plump' for new men who were of known experience and ability. Phipps understood navigation and Delaval had established at nearby Seaton Sluice glass-houses, copperas works and brickyards with capital from his brother, Sir John Delaval. In the event, tradition proved too strong. The only companies where a majority favoured Phipps and Delaval were the butchers, joiners, and bricklayers. Namier includes Newcastle as a parliamentary constituency relatively immune from corruption at elections. It should be noted that national politics were relatively unimportant and that both Blackett and his opponent Phipps were strong supporters of George III.

THE END OF THE UNREFORMED CORPORATION

The early nineteenth century saw increasing resentment that political power should lie in the hands of a wealthy few. In Newcastle the corporation derived handsome revenues from the ballast shores that lined the river, amounting in 1826 to £19,681. Tolls and various quay dues raised a further £9,223, and rents and fines produced £8,687. During his term of office the mayor lived in a handsome Mansion House in the Close and entertained royally on his allowance of £2,000. Standing charges included repairs to property (£5,245), public amenities including street cleansing (£11,582), salaries (£7,919) and hospital provision (£1,321). This same year of 1826, while receipts totalled £42,959 9s 9d, expenditure topped £44,799 12s 10d.

Dissatisfaction in the town slowly crystallised around the

movement for parliamentary reform, perhaps from the belief that the corporation was incapable of change from within its ranks. The ringleaders were John Fife, a local surgeon and co-founder of the Newcastle Eye Infirmary (1822), Dr T. E. Headlam, a physician at the Newcastle Infirmary, Thomas Doubleday, pamphleteer and secretary of the Northern Political Union, Charles Attwood, promoter of the Weardale Iron and Coal Company (based at Tow Law) and James Losh, a barrister. Meetings were called to advocate parliamentary reform, wider educational opportunities, abolition of slavery, Catholic emancipation and free trade. The first Reform Act, passed in June 1832, gave Gateshead, South Shields and Tynemouth each a representative in parliament. New parliamentary elections were held in December 1832. The sitting members for Newcastle again presented themselves, but Charles Attwood agreed to stand against them on the programme of household suffrage, a secret ballot, triennial parliaments, the abolition of the Tithe Tax, the repeal of the Corn Laws and corporation reform. The Reform Act had enlarged Newcastle's electorate from a supposed 3,000 freemen to an approximate 5,000 householders. The total population in 1831 was 53,613. Despite popular enthusiasm the electorate was cautious and Attwood polled only 1,092 votes against the 2,105 and 1,678 polled by Sir Matthew White Ridley and John Hodgson respectively. Attwood expressed his feelings bitterly. 'It is not merely to Tory corruption and Corporation speculators that you, gentlemen, and your unrepresented fellow-townsmen are indebted for your late defeat . . . assisted as they have been by threatening or cajoling parsons, by intimidating tyrant-masters, and Puritans whose canting cadences distil so suitably from lying lips. No, gentlemen, it is the false reformers whose apostate voices have determined the victory in favour of corruption and of mock reform.' Possibly he had in mind the appointment of James Losh by the corporation as recorder of Newcastle.

The Newcastle reformers now turned specifically to reform of the corporation. At the Michaelmas guild day of 1833 John Fife led the attack, denouncing the newly introduced police force as 'the mere tools of a political oligarchy, the instruments of tyranny, and the panderers of corruption'. He also alleged widespread nepotism and other abuses.

Irrespective of local agitation, there was a national mood to break the power of the closed municipal corporations. In 1833 a royal commission was appointed to examine boroughs throughout England and Wales, and in accordance with its terms of reference Fortunatus Dwarris and Sampson Augustus Rumball, two of the commissioners, summoned before them in the Newcastle Guildhall on 31 October 1833 the various town officers and representatives of interested parties. Proceedings lasted until 10 November, by which date the commissioners had also heard the claims of Gateshead to be considered as a corporation. The result was inevitable, because the commissioners as convinced Benthamites were certain that household franchise would cure all municipal ills. Although Newcastle had a good record for public health, street improvement, and schools and hospitals for the poor, it was included in the Municipal Corporations Act of 1835. This decreed that henceforth the town should be governed by a council consisting of a mayor, sheriff, fourteen aldermen and a body of forty-two councillors, the latter elected for a term of three years by the rate-paying householders. At the same time the town boundaries were extended to include the adjacent townships of Westgate, Elswick, Jesmond, Heaton and Byker.

SELECT BIBLIOGRAPHY

J. BAILLIE   *An Impartial History of Newcastle and its Vicinity* (Newcastle, 1801)

F. W. DENDY   'The Struggle between the Merchant and Craft Guilds of Newcastle in 1515' (*Arch Ael* 3rd ser VII, 1911)

C. M. FRASER   'The life and death of John of Denton' (*Arch Ael* 4th ser XXXVII, 1959)

C. M. FRASER and K. EMSLEY   'Some Early Recorders of Newcastle upon Tyne' (*Arch Ael* 4th ser XLIX, 1971)

C. M. F<small>RASER</small>
and K. E<small>MSLEY</small>
W. H. D. L<small>ONGSTAFFE</small> (ed)
L. N<small>AMIER</small>

'Justice in North East England, 1256–1356' (*The American Journal of Legal History*, vol XV, 1971)
Memoirs of Ambrose Barnes (Surtees Soc 50, 1866)
The Structure of Politics at the Accession of George III (1957, 2nd edition)

Chapter 5 AFFLUENCE AND
SQUALOR

GEORGIAN TYNESIDE

THE peculiar fascination of Georgian Tyne-
side lies in its diversity. There were the rich like Ralph Carr, who
was worth on his death in 1807 over £100,000: there were the
very poor, dependent on casual charity, whose plight was noted
only when general famine gripped Tyneside, as in 1739-40. There
were the artistically gifted, such as Thomas Bewick, who still is
acknowledged as master of the art of English wood-engraving, and
David Stephenson, architect of the finest Georgian parish church
in England—All Saints, Newcastle. There were the glass-blowers
who produced exquisite crystal, to be decorated with engraving
by John Challinge or with enamel by William and Mary Beilby.
The Newcastle Assay Office, re-established there in 1702, is estimated to have passed an average of 12,500oz of silver each year
during this period; and no fewer than seventy-eight silversmiths
were registered with their marks. There was money on Tyneside,
and people with taste to demand the best that money could buy.

On the other hand, money derived mainly from coal and industry presupposes a large working population. From the mouth
of the Tyne to Newburn, the banks of the river were lined with
salt-pans, glass-houses, slipways, rope-walks, ballast shores, iron-
works, timber-yards and the like. Working on the river were the
keel-men, on whom the colliery owners depended to keep coal
shipments moving, and the seamen who manned the ships which
carried Baltic rye to keep bread in the Tyneside workers' bellies,
lead sheathing for Burmese temples, iron shovels for the American
plantations, and coal wherever there was a market.

CROWLEY IRON WORKS

Ambrose Crowley came of an established family of ironware manufacturers at Stourbridge in Worcestershire. He had keen business instincts, and to break the stranglehold on prices exercised by the Stourbridge nail-makers, he established, before 1685 at Sunderland, a nail-factory where Swedish iron was used by workers introduced from Liège and other continental iron-centres. His distribution point was London and his main customers the Thames ship-building yards and the Admiralty, so that he estimated that sea-transport from Sunderland was as speedy as land-transport from Birmingham. When his Catholic workers were mobbed by Sunderland inhabitants for their religion, he decided to build his own community in the country beside the Derwent. He leased a disused cornmill and some land at Winlaton in April 1691, and from the manufacture of nails, which brought him naval contracts from 1693, extended to pots, hinges, wheel-hubs, hatchets, anchors and finally cannons. Steel furnaces and a slitting-mill were added by 1703. Harnessing the water-power of the Derwent, Crowley's works later spread to Swalwell and Teams, and included forges, two foundries, rolling- and slitting-mills and cementation furnaces. The factory complex was as noteworthy, however, for its social organisation as for its size and for its output of ironware, which was of international reputation.

Crowley's works was a strange mixture of cottage industry and factory supervision. The bar-iron was produced in factory conditions, after which it was issued to the smiths in sufficient quantity to last for a week's work. The smiths then had to appear with the finished product of nails, shovels and the like, and any surplus iron, which was checked; and they were fined for any apparent deficiency. The accumulation of fines, less the proportion paid to informers, provided a fund from which were drawn benefits in sickness, old age, unemployment or funeral expenses. A physician was in attendance at the factory from 1724, to prescribe for 'my honest and laborious workmen and their families when visited with sickness and other bodily infirmities . . .', and his services were free to those entitled to them. The workers' children were to attend school daily, in winter from 8am to noon and from 1pm to 4pm, and in summer from 6am to 11am and from 1pm to 5pm. Holidays were limited to church festivals. The master was to teach his pupils the catechism and 'to take care to make his scholars shew due respects to their superiors and especially aged persons, and to correct such as he finds guilty of lying, swearing or such like horrid crimes, but above all things set a good example before the children himself, example availing more than precept'. The Law Book of the Crowley Iron Works, preserving these minute rules, is regarded as a unique record of patriarchal industrialism.

Crowley strove for complete self-sufficiency. He imported his own bar-iron from places as distant as Russia, Sweden and America. Once the metal had reached the Tyne, he collected it in wagons, drawn by horses supplied by his own farm stables. The blacksmiths used coal from Crowley collieries to heat the iron for working. The finished products were taken to his warehouse at Blaydon, whence they were shipped by keel and Crowley-owned coastal vessels to the head office at Greenwich. An interesting sidelight on this community is that Wesley apparently rarely visited it. For a century 'Crowley's Crew' were staunch Anglicans, under the influence of their works chaplain. Eventually they fell from grace, and by the early nineteenth century were famed not only for their epic fights with the blacksmiths from the rival ironworks of Hawks, Crawshay of Gateshead, but also for their militant radicalism. The works was finally closed about 1860, in the face of competition from the newly founded iron and steel works of Middlesborough; but in its heyday Crowley's works had been the main production centre in England for 'shear steel'. This was the material from which high-grade cutlery was fashioned. By a successive process of heating and hammering, bar-iron was forged into steel for cloth shears and in still harder form for making penknives, fine scissors, razors and engraving tools. Crowley's product was regarded as superior to contemporary German steel made in Styria and the Tyrol, and previously imported in large quantities. Sheffield did not seize the leadership in English steel-making until Benjamin Huntsman had invented cast or crucible steel and his son established himself there in business in 1787.

Ambrose Crowley and his heirs were untypical of Tyneside industrialists, not in their concern for their workers' welfare, but because they were outsiders from Worcestershire and conducted their business from London. Such wealth as they amassed left Tyneside and played no part in the local cultural scene. Very different were the mine-owning Blacketts of Newcastle, who for four generations dominated the Newcastle political scene.

BLACKETT FAMILY

The founder of the Blackett fortunes was William, a member of the Newcastle Company of Merchant Adventurers, who was admitted to the Company of Hostmen in 1652 and became alderman of Newcastle in 1660, mayor in 1666, and member of Parliament in 1673. His mining interests embraced six collieries on Tyneside and lead mines in East and West Allendale and in Alston Moor. Later, in 1676, he bought from his parliamentary colleague, Henry Anderson, the great mansion within the town walls known successively as Newe Place and Anderson House, and there on 16 May 1680 he died.

William Blackett II, the third surviving son, inherited his father's business interests in Newcastle and immediately entered politics, being elected successively between 1683 and 1685 mayor, governor of the Hostmen's Company, and member of parliament. About 1690 Blackett established himself as a county landowner by buying the debt-encumbered estates of Wallington and Hexham from Sir John Fenwick, a fervent adherent of James II, who was beheaded on Tower Hill in January 1697 for complicity in plots to assassinate William III. On his death in London in December 1705, where he was attending parliament, Blackett's body was brought back for burial in St Nicholas's church at a total cost in funeral expenses of £688 14s, including £127 13s 6d spent on 1,285 pairs of gloves distributed to mourners. In his will Sir William, a baronet since 1684, left £1,000 to form a trust whose income was to be divided into three portions, of which the first should be used to bind poor apprentices in Newcastle, the second distributed to poor householders in the parish of St Andrew, and the third to pay a schoolmaster to teach thirty poor children of that parish to read and to memorise the Church Catechism.

Sir William Blackett III inherited his father's wealth but not his business abilities. He represented Newcastle in parliament from 1710 to 1728 and was a member of the Hostmen's Company, of which he became governor, like his father and grandfather; but he was believed to favour the cause of the Old Pretender. When in 1718 he sought election as mayor of Newcastle, he required letters from London certifying that he was loyal to the House of Hanover. As at his death in 1728 he had no family by his wife, his property descended to his nephew Walter Calverley on the understanding that he married Blackett's illegitimate daughter Elizabeth.

Sir Walter Calverley Blackett (the baronetcy being a Calverley inheritance) had a full measure of ancestral business acumen. His agent reported in 1731 that the Blackett land scarcely paid for itself, but 'the lead mines have turned to very great account'. Two years later he estimated that land, mines and collieries were averaging a clear yearly income of between £4,000 and £5,000. Lead, moreover, was entering a period of rising prices. In 1734 lead fetched £11 14s 11d a ton, but by 1754 the price had risen to £16 3s 1d a ton. Having established his finances, Sir Walter presented himself successfully for parliamentary election in 1734. In the following year he was elected mayor of Newcastle, an office which he held again in 1748, 1756, 1764 and 1771.

During the exceptionally cold winter of 1739–40, when the Tyne froze and shipping was halted, Blackett gave £350 to be distributed among the poor of Newcastle and Gateshead, earning himself the title of Father of the Poor. He donated a further £100 during the grain shortage of 1757. He founded an almshouse in the Manors in 1754 for the maintenance of six 'poor and decayed burgesses'. He was a generous benefactor to Newcastle Infirmary, founded in 1751, of which he was a governor. Each birthday he caused a distribution to be made to the poor of beef, bread and money.

KEELMEN

Turning now to the poor, the most obvious candidates for benevolence were the keelmen. Their labour in ferrying coal from the staithes to the sea-going colliers was essential to preserve the momentum of the coal-trade. This labour was physically punishing, and men were unfit for work when they reached their forties. In consequence, there was a residue of unemployable keelmen in Sandgate, chargeable on the poor rate of All Saints, in addition to the widows and orphaned children. Mindful of the needs of their brethren, there was a movement among the keelmen in 1699 to establish a provident fund through the compulsory deduction by their employers, the Newcastle Hostmen, of 1d a tide from the wages of the keel-crew. The Stewards of the Hostmen's Company were to act as trustees as the keelmen, being unincorporated, had no legal standing. The Newcastle corporation put at their disposal land in Sandgate, on which in 1701 a Keelmen's Hospital was built at a cost of over £2,000. Accommodation in the hospital consisted of fifty 'chambers' giving on to a cloister walk enclosing a grass court. By 1788 supplementary relief for the keelmen came from the fund in the form of allowances of 5s a week for the disabled, lame and sick; 3s a week for the aged; 1s 6d for widows and those widows who had one child, and 2s for widows with two or more children.

Even the able-bodied keelmen had difficulties to overcome. There was the covert trade practice of the Hostmen of offering over-measure both to evade the customs-house and also to compete with rival coal fitters. In consequence, the customary 'keel-load' grew in volume from 16 tons in 1600 to 21 tons 4cwt in 1695, when the chaldron measure was fixed by statute at 53cwt. Even so, during the eighteenth century, the hold of the keel was illegally enlarged from the traditional eight chaldrons to contain ten chaldrons, equal to 26 tons 10cwt. This meant that the keel-crew, paid by the journey, had to work longer and harder to fill the hold for the same wages, part of which were paid in drink, to be consumed in 'can-houses' owned by the employers. Contrary winds as well as ice on the river closed the Tyne to coal shipments during the winter, when the men were paid off. Some returned home to Scotland. Others, who stayed, were ineligible for parish relief because under the terms of the Elizabethan Poor Law Act of 1601 relief was paid only where a person had 'settlement', that is where he was born or had recognised employment. Work under bond of less than a year did not provide 'settlement', and the keelmen's work being seasonal did not qualify. Their plight was depicted in a letter of George Liddel, a Gateshead coalowner, whose humanity required him to protest against a proposal to shorten the sailing-season still further, to raise prices on the London market.

> What must become of the poor keelmen? They are the Sort of Unthinking people that spend their money as fast, nay generally before they get it. They give over work the beginning of November and many of them had not then a shilling before hand. They live upon their Credit and a little labouring work till they get their binding money at Christmas. That money goes to their Creditors and then they borrow of their fitters to buy provisions and have credit with the Runners for a little Drink and so they put off till trade begins which is generally about Candlemas [2 February]. Now, if they are not to begin till about Ladyday [25 March], half of them will be starved; for as their time of working will be so much shorter trades' people will not trust them, there being no prospect of being repaid.

To remedy their grievances the keelmen repeatedly went on strike. In 1710 they protested on account of their low wages: in 1719 and 1744 over 'overmeasure'. In a strike of 1750 which lasted over seven weeks the grievances were 'overmeasure', 'can-money', moving coal at the staithes, and unwarrantable delays before they could load or unload. Further strikes occurred in 1768, 1771, 1809, 1819, and a culminating strike lasting ten weeks in 1822. The keelmen realised that they could disrupt the supply of coal to London, and to that extent could be exceedingly troublesome to their employers. On the other hand, the funds controlled by the Keelmen's Hospital were kept firmly in Host-men's hands lest they be used as 'strike benefit'. The keelmen's meagre resources could not support a strike of significant duration. A short stoppage enhanced prices when deliveries were resumed— to the profit of the coal-suppliers. With the introduction in 1822 of steam power on the river in the form of paddle-tugs, the need for keelmen gradually diminished. Their use disappeared entirely as dredging, and the replacement of the low-level Tyne bridge by a swing-bridge in 1876, enabled ships of all draughts to load directly at staithes even as far up river as Dunston.

The keelmen, mostly living in Sandgate, Newcastle, must be regarded as more characteristic Tyneside workers even than the pitmen. In his traditional 'Sunday best' of short blue jacket, slate-coloured and bell-bottomed trousers, yellow waistcoat, white shirt and blue bonnet the keelman passed into folklore.

> As I came through Sandgate, through Sandgate, through Sandgate,
>   I heard a lassie sing,
> Weel may the keel row, that my laddie's in.
>
> He wears a blue bonnet, blue bonnet, blue bonnet,
>   A dimple in his chin.
> Weel may the keel row, that my laddie's in.

The keelmen were claimed by the Royal Navy as a reserve to serve in times of emergency, although in practice the press gangs of the eighteenth century were only allowed to operate among them when they showed signs of preparing for a strike.

SEAMEN

The other pool of men for naval service were the sea-going colliermen, equally protected against the press gangs while busy on coal-shipments; although we have another relevant ditty, com-memorating John Bover, post captain and 'regulating officer' of the port of Newcastle.

> Where hes ti' been, maw canny hinny?
> Where hes ti' been, maw winsome man?
> Aw've been ti' the norrard,

E

> Cruising back and forrard,
> Aw've been ti' the norrard,
> Cruising sair and lang,
> Aw've been ti' the norrard,
> Cruising back and forrard,
> But daurna come ashore
> For Bover and his gang.

The hazards of seafaring led to a steep increase in seamen's wages; it being asserted in 1702 that a boy of seventeen could earn 46s a month and a man £7 or £8 a voyage, against a previous 30s. When the shippers sought to depress these rates, the seamen went on strike and had to be coerced by the militia to return to work. In February 1793, at the outbreak of the Revolutionary Wars, the local seamen captured a press gang at North Shields. Reversing the men's jackets, the seamen escorted them out of the district, warning them never again to enter Shields 'under pain of being torn limb from limb'. When in 1796 the seamen struck for higher wages, the ringleaders were handed over to the press gang.

Another occupational hazard was shipwreck. The Black Midden Rocks and Herd Sand exacted a heavy toll, leading to the offer in 1789 of a reward of two guineas for any plan for a boat capable of containing twenty-four persons in a 'very shoal heavy broken sea'. Henry Greathead of South Shields submitted such a model and obtained contracts to build a number of these lifeboats for ports both at home and abroad. The South Shields lifeboat made its first rescue from the Herd Sand on 30 January 1790. Additional dangers were capture by French privateers and incarceration in a French prison. Out of one convoy of coal ships, bound for London early in 1800, only two of the seventy-one reached their destination. It was estimated that by 1792 8,000 seamen were engaged in the coal-trade, with a further 946 yard-workers keeping the ships in repair.

JOHN WESLEY

To this working population of keelmen, seamen and others in

the glass-houses and factories along the river came John Wesley in May 1742. 'We came to Newcastle about six, and after a short refreshment walked into the town. I was surprised; so much drunkenness, cursing and swearing (even from the mouths of little children) do I never remember to have seen and heard before, in so small a compass of time'. At 7am on Sunday, 30 May, Wesley 'walked down to Sand-Gate, the poorest and most contemptible part of the town', and having attracted a crowd by the singing of the 100th psalm, he preached an extempore sermon to what he estimated as about 1,500 people. He returned that evening, to find the slope reaching up to the Keelmen's Hospital 'covered from top to bottom. . . After preaching, the poor people were ready to tread me under foot, out of pure love and kindness'.

Wesley returned to Tyneside on 13 November 1742 and preached the following evening in the 'Square' of the Keelmen's Hospital. He was somewhat perplexed by the way his words were received this time, for though numbers were great there appeared a general apathy. He was equally nonplussed when later he was clapped on the back by Pelton coal-miners, 'their usual token of approbation'. Nevertheless, Wesley decided to found a meeting-house at Newcastle, and early in December bought a plot of ground off Northumberland Street. Here was built the Orphan House, the second building to be erected specifically for Methodist meetings. The first was the New Room at Bristol in 1739. On 5 March 1745 the Orphan House was formally entrusted to various local preachers to provide 'a centre for evangelical effort in the northern districts: a home for itinerant helpers in the work of the ministry: and a possible place of instruction for the children of the destitute poor'. This latter project was not realised before 1790, when a Sunday-school was opened.

Wesley recorded in his journal vivid sketches of conditions on Tyneside. At Chowdean, a colliery village beside Gateshead, 'I found we were got into the very Kingswood of the North. Twenty or thirty wild children ran around us, as soon as we came, staring as in amaze'. At another such village, Plessey, 'Their grand assembly used to be on the Lord's Day, on which men, women, and children met together, to dance, fight, curse, and swear, and play at chuck-ball, span-farthing, or whatever came next to hand'. On a later visit in May 1755 Wesley commended the newly founded Newcastle Infirmary. 'It is finely situated on the top of a hill, and is the best ordered of any place of the kind I have seen in England. Nor did I ever see so much seriousness in a hospital before. . .' Under 4 June 1758, Wesley wrote, 'Certainly if I did not believe there was another world, I should spend all my summers here [ie at Newcastle], as I know no place in Great Britain comparable to it for pleasantness'.

Wesley, in his enthusiasm for saving souls, may have looked on the numerous inhabitants of Tyneside as a particularly promising harvest-field and cared little for its cultural amenities. Yet in the eighteenth century Newcastle was the social centre for Northumberland as well as Tyneside; and the assize weeks attracted county gentry to their town houses and opened theatres and concert halls. In the days of poor road communications, when it took two days to travel by mail coach between Newcastle and London—and this service was not introduced before 1786—regions had to be self-sufficient.

GLASS TRADE

The Tyneside glass-making industry had started about 1623 with Mansell's works to the east of the mouth of the Ouseburn, making bottles, window-glass, mirror-glass, tumblers and spectacle glass. Fine quality glassware was not manufactured locally until the establishment in 1684 by the Dagnia brothers from Bristol of a glasshouse outside Closegate. Their glass was characterised by a brilliant clarity, produced by the introduction of lead into the 'metal' from which the glass was made. Their wine glasses had long, slender stems with several 'knops' or bulges in which tears like little icicles dripped downwards. This glass was particularly suitable for engraving, and Newcastle specimens, decorated in diamond point, may be found in the Victoria and Albert Museum and other collections. The leading Newcastle engravers were John and Samuel Challinge and John Williams; while William and

Mary Beilby, brother and sister, decorated their glasses in white enamel with scenes of shooting, fishing, hunting, skating, country walks and picturesque ruins. While Beilby glasses were the aristocrats of the lead-glass trade, cheap soda glass was also produced on Tyneside, particularly for 'Jacobite glasses' in honour of the exiled House of Stuart.

The glass trade was a by-product of the coal trade. Cheap local coal melted the 'metal', while the sand and flint to provide silica, the basic material, were imported as ballast in the collier-fleet. Potash in its various forms was similarly imported. The manufactured glassware was packed in crates and stowed amongst the coal for distribution to its markets in London and abroad. Matthew Ridley of Heaton Hall, lessee of collieries at Tanfield and Byker, acquired the Howdon Pans glass works from the Henzell family in 1759. Earlier, his father-in-law, Matthew White of Blagdon, with coal interests at Willington, Jesmond and Blaydon, had dabbled in glass-houses as an outlet for his coal. In 1765 Sir Matthew White Ridley, their heir, is described as one of the principal bottle-makers on Tyneside.

By the beginning of the eighteenth century the Tyne glass works had expanded from Closegate (Dagnia Brothers), Ouseburn (Mansell) and Howdon (Henzell) to South Shields, where John and Onesiphorus Dagnia had established glass-houses before 1712. They may have been preceded at South Shields by Isaac Cookson, whose speciality was blown plate glass for windows. John Cookson, Isaac's son, diversified his interests by manufacturing alum at South Shields for use in his glass works. Gateshead was comparatively late in the manufacture of glass, its first recorded works being on the Salt Meadows. The business of George Sowerby was established at New Stourbridge in Gateshead in 1760. By 1772, there were on Tyneside five houses for the manufacture of broad window glass, five for glass bottles, three for crown glass for windows, two for flint glass, and one for plate glass. The glass works at Lemington near Newburn was established about 1780 by the Northumberland Glass Company, whose partners included Sir Matthew White Ridley and members of the Henzel and Tyzack families. This superseded the glass-houses at Howdon Pans and the high and low glass-works in Closegate, Newcastle.

BANKING

Considerable capital was involved in these industrial ventures, and recourse was made to goldsmiths and lawyers for loans. Pitmen, glassworkers, keelmen, and other labouring men required their wages in cash at a time when coin was becoming more difficult to acquire. The same problem arose when the government of George II needed to pay troops stationed at Newcastle at the time of the Jacobite rebellion of 1745. This emergency was met by Ralph Carr, a general merchant in Newcastle, whose overseas interests ranged from the American plantations to the Far East. According to Sir Lewis Namier, government contracts were of invaluable assistance to overseas traders, as they ensured a certain demand for the named commodity and an equally sure payment. The contracts also ensured that the merchant would have large sums of money on hand, with which he could engage in short-term finance for his own profit. When Ralph Carr acted as government banker of troop payments in 1745 this was but one step in a business career which had begun in 1737. Carr traded in coals and iron, logwood and corn, glass and alum, wines and spirits, butter and tea, tobacco and snuff. He was also an insurance broker for ships. In 1755 he took the important decision to open a banking-house for the receipt of money for deposit, maintenance of current accounts, discounting of bills of exchange, and transfer of money by draft on London agents. With the possible exception of the banking-house of Samuel Smith of Nottingham, Carr's bank was the first to be constituted outside London.

The bank premises were in Lower Pilgrim Street near All Saints' church. Carr brought into partnership Matthew Bell, who was a Hostman and brother-in-law of Matthew Ridley, John Cookson of the Close Gate and South Shields glass-houses, and Joseph Airey, a corn-miller. From August 1755 they issued their own banknotes, which in 1757 were declared acceptable tender by the

Collector of Excise. By 1774 the firm had a note issue of £180,000, cash and bills in hand totalling £103,597, deposits with other bankers of £47,860, navy bills worth £14,609, overdrafts worth £38,000, and deposits exceeding £85,000. Trading profits that year amounted to £5,712. After 1768, with the establishment of the Exchange Bank at Newcastle by Aubone Surtees and Rowland Burdon, the partnership of Bell, Cookson, Carr and Airey was known as the 'Old Bank'; and later, when Sir Matthew White Ridley had succeeded on Carr's retirement in 1787, as Ridley and Company. By 1800 Newcastle had four banks, not counting the Commercial Bank, whose life spanned from 1784 to 1793, when a run on gold during a monetary panic caused it to suspend payments and discontinue business.

It is interesting to find that these banks were issuing their own notes for denominations ranging from £1 to 5 guineas. By 1793 there was paper money in circulation to the value of £230,000. Hard on their trail came the forger, and the advice of Newcastle's most distinguished wood-engraver, Thomas Bewick, was sought to devise a block which would defy imitation.

BOOK TRADE AND THOMAS BEWICK
The *Newcastle Courant* was the first provincial newspaper to be published north of the Trent, beginning publication in 1712. The previous year John White, son of the 'royal printer' of William III, set up his printing press and continued for fifty years, printing and publishing sermons, histories and ballads. Towards the end of his life White took into partnership Thomas Saint, and from 1762 they printed and published the treatises on mensuration of Dr Charles Hutton, then a local schoolmaster but subsequently professor of mathematics at Woolwich Academy and a Fellow of the Royal Society. Saint employed the firm of Ralph Beilby, engraver, to supply the illustrations to these and other books, particularly fables and educational works for children. The actual blocks were engraved by Beilby's apprentice, Thomas Bewick, who took up a partnership with his old master in 1777.

During these years Newcastle was a centre of the printing trade.

Fig 4 'Laid Up' (Bewick vignette)

Its output of children's books was larger than any other city save London. Its printing houses also specialised in sermons, Wesleyan tracts and practical handbooks. Bewick was of a serious turn of mind, and in 1790 issued, in partnership with Ralph Beilby, a *General History of Quadrupeds*, the text being largely written by Beilby and the illustrations by Bewick. This was followed by a *History of British Birds*, published in two volumes in 1797 and in 1804. The *Birds* is generally acknowledged to be Bewick's masterpiece, not only for his understanding of the birds and their habitat, but also for his tailpieces to each section. These scenes from country life and pastimes or bizarre drolleries have been likened to the medieval misericords—or the glass enamellings of William Beilby, brother of Bewick's partner. Ruskin described Bewick as 'the Burns of painting'.

Fig 5 'Loading Coal at the Staithes' (Bewick vignette)

HOUSING

In the days before railways, workers and employers had to live close to their place of business. In the first quarter of the eighteenth century, Westgate in Newcastle was a select residential street 'chiefly inhabited by the Clergy and Gentry'. The elegant new Assembly Rooms, designed by a local architect, William Newton, was sited there in 1776. The northern part of the town between Newgate and Pilgrim Street Gate was largely occupied by the mansion house and grounds of the Blacketts. Off the east side of Pilgrim Street lay the Carliol Croft, forming 'a very agreeable walk, generally frequented in a Summer's Evening by the Gentry of this Part of the Town; The Prospect of the Gardens, some of which are exceeding Curious, affording a good deal of Pleasure'. Mid-Pilgrim Street was noteworthy for the 'very pretty, neat, and regular' houses of the town's leading businessmen, such as Nicholas Fenwick and Matthew White (Fenwick's house still stands). New houses were being built on the site of the old White Friars at Hanover Square and outside the walls along Gallowgate and Northumberland Street. Already the merchants had largely deserted the Close for the higher part of the town, although the mayor's official residence remained there till it was sold by the reformed corporation in 1836.

The Sandhill, however, maintained its position as the centre of trade and business, adjacent to the Guildhall. Aubone Surtees, of the banking partnership of Surtees and Burdon, continued to live over his premises on the Sandhill until the scandalous elopement in 1772 of his daughter Bessie with John Scott, the son of a Newcastle Hostman. Thereafter the stares of sightseers forced Surtees to move to the quieter neighbourhood of Newgate. Scott, by his exertions at the Bar, subsequently rose to be Lord Chancellor of England (1801–6 and 1807–27) and earl of Eldon.

To minister to the spiritual needs of the increasing population along the North Shore, the chapel of St Anne had been rebuilt in 1768 to the designs of William Newton, from the stones of the now demolished stretch of town wall along the Quayside. The

73

New or City Road was built past the Keelmen's Hospital in 1776 to provide a direct turnpike route from Pandon Gate to Heaton and North Shields, avoiding the steepness of Pandon Bank.

Around St Andrew's church were some of the poorer parts, inhabited by the artisans of Newcastle. It was in one of these cottages, in High Friar Lane, that Richard Grainger, the builder, was born in 1797. Below All Saints' church lay Sandgate, 'more crowded with inhabitants than any other place within or without the walls of Newcastle, containing many thousand souls'. Forty years later, Mackenzie observed in 1827 that the lanes of Sandgate 'are in general dark, narrow, ill paved, and noisome'. The industrial character of the neighbourhoods was underlined by the stinking tanneries beside St Andrew or the limekilns and shipyards of Sandgate. Westwards along the riverbank, the Close had become equally industrialised, merchants' houses being replaced by glass-warehouses in addition to the glass-factories of Dagnia and Cookson and an iron foundry. Defoe had commented in 1722 on the 'prodigious number' of poor in the town; and poor relief in the parish of All Saints, which included Sandgate, had been institutionalised before 1785. (In Gateshead a Poor House had been approved and built by the church-wardens by 1755.)

SCHOOLS

Poor relief was well organised in comparison with provision of education, even for the children of the well-to-do. The Royal Grammar School, re-established successively by Thomas Horsley in 1540 and Queen Elizabeth in 1600, was under the patronage of Newcastle corporation and its curriculum limited to the study of Latin and Greek. Private academies had sporadic existence under particular masters such as Charles Hutton the mathematician. Trinity House provided in 1712 a free school for the instruction of the children and apprentices of its members. Individual benefactors such as Mrs Eleanor Allan bequeathed to particular churches rents to be used for teaching children of the parish. The school so attached to St Nicholas took boys from the ages of eight to twelve, educating them for apprenticeships in the town or at sea. The average number of boys in each establishment was forty. The first Sunday School was started by the Rev William Turner at the Hanover Square Unitarian Chapel in 1784. The first Methodist Sunday School opened at the Orphan House in Northumberland Street in 1790, when 1,012 children enrolled as pupils to learn to read the bible.

Even including tutors and private schools, only a tiny proportion of the population of Newcastle received any formal education. As for the rest of Tyneside, there was the Anchorage School at Gateshead, endowed in 1701 to teach fifteen boys, and a charity school at South Shields founded in 1772 to teach forty scholars. There are brief references to parish schools at North Shields and at Wallsend.

WATER SUPPLY

Another amenity in short supply for rich and poor alike was water. There are references in the town chamberlains' accounts of the reign of Queen Elizabeth to public 'pants' or cisterns, and their repair at the corporation's expense. The main sources were springs on the Town Moor and at Pandon, which fed by conduit the public fountains, each of which had a trough in front for the use of horses. In 1694 new springs were tapped on Castle Leazes, and three years later pipes were laid to bring water from Gateshead Fell. In 1748 and 1777 action was taken to increase supplies from north and west of Newcastle, with provision in 1770 for fire-plugs for emergency use.

Gateshead, which supplied water to Newcastle and had from the twelfth century a district known as Pipewellgate (traditionally so called from the pipes bringing water to it from the higher ground), itself relied at the end of the eighteenth century on a few wells. Shipping needs for ale prompted six brewers in North Shields to obtain incorporation by private act of parliament in 1786 to take water from three reservoirs, the one nearest the New Quay being picturesquely named Waterville. At South Shields a water company was incorporated in 1787 to supply both domestic consumers and also brewers, beer retailers and licensed victuallers. The water was brought from Caldwell Springs to the south of Westoe by wooden pipes consisting of the hollowed trunks of young trees. These drained into a reservoir from which the water was distributed by barrels mounted on wheels. Pants were not introduced until a later date.

CONCLUSIONS

During the eighteenth century Newcastle started to shake itself free of its medieval inheritance of town walls and municipal administration in leading strings to the wholesale guildsmen. A spirit of self-improvement was stirring, as shown in the Keelmen's Hospital, financed by the Keelmen, the conversions to Methodism, the group of Unitarian merchants with their new chapel in Hanover Square, and lastly in the body of radicals and scientists who banded together in 1793 to form the Literary and Philosophical Society as a forum for discussion of all kinds of knowledge —barring religion, law, medicine and politics.

SELECT BIBLIOGRAPHY

H. BOURNE	*History of Newcastle* (1736)
R. E. CARR	*History of the Family of Carr* (1893)
M. W. FLINN	*Men of Iron* (Edinburgh, 1962)
J. HODGSON	*History of Northumberland*, Part II, vol I (1827)
M. PHILLIPS	*Bankers and Banking in Northumberland, Durham and North Yorkshire* (1894)
A. SCHUBERT	*History of the British Iron and Steel Industry* (1957)
R. SURTEES	*History of the County of Durham*, ii (1820)
W. A. THORPE	*English Glass* (1935)
M. WEEKLEY	*Thomas Bewick* (Oxford, 1953)
J. WESLEY	*Journals*
J. M. FEWSTER	'The Keelmen of Tyneside in the 18th Century' (*Durham University Journal*, New Series, vol XIX, 1957–8)
U. RIDLEY	'The History of Glassmaking on the Tyne and Wear' (*Arch Ael* 4th ser XL, 1962)

Chapter 6   THE AGE OF STEAM

For much of England the 'Age of Steam' means the coming of the railways. Elsewhere it indicates the abandonment of water power in favour of steam, as in the cotton and woollen towns of Lancashire and Yorkshire. On Tyneside the age of steam begins with the Newcomen pumping engine, introduced in the 1720s; reaches maturity with George and Robert Stephenson, their locomotives and permanent way; and culminates in steamships including the *Mauretania*. In each case the steam in the boiler was coal-heated, and in each case progress in engineering was harnessed to the needs of the coal trade.

TYNESIDE WAGONWAYS

As early as 1689 it was claimed that on Tyneside 'the coalpits nearest the water are almost quite exhausted and decayed'. In consequence, it was necessary to dig for coal at some distance from the river, using for transport a special track of parallel wooden rails laid on sleepers, along which a horse could draw a wagon with flanged wheels containing a load of about 33½cwt. Apart from a line near Bedlington, the earliest known 'Newcastle wagon road', as the device became known throughout England, was between Ravensworth and the staithes at Team, where the coal was loaded into keels for trans-shipment. This Ravensworth wagonway was certainly working by 1671. To facilitate haulage, 'wherever there are any hills or vales between colliery and the river and the same cannot be avoided, it is necessary . . . to make cuts through the hills or level the same, and to raise or fill up the vales so that such wagon ways may lye upon a level as near as possible'. The Tanfield wagonway, built about

1725, included an embankment 100ft high and 300ft broad at the base, and a single-span bridge, the Causey Arch, 105ft long and 80ft high. Additional expense arose from 'wayleaves' imposed in the form of royalties payable to owners of land over which the wagonway might pass. The alternative to such massive costs in civil engineering was to mine coal nearer the Tyne but at greater depths.

Although the High Main seam outcropped on Newcastle Town Moor, at Wallsend it lay 666ft and at Gosforth 1,134ft underground. The lowest or Brockwell seam lay 2,000ft below the High Main. The coal-owners faced formidable problems of drainage, haulage and ventilation if they attempted to mine from the lower coal measures. A common form of drainage was the endless chain, to which buckets were attached. The driving wheel was moved either by water power or by horses, which precluded a depth of more than 360ft. The atmospheric pumps of Savory and Newcomen brought new hope for collieries where 'feeders' or springs were seeping into the mine galleries. The coals when hewn from the coal-face had to be dragged in corves or baskets to the base of the mine shaft and again hauled to the surface by a horse-driven whim gin. If the air in the galleries did not circulate, pockets would form of 'fire-damp' or methane and of its even more deadly companion, 'choke-damp' or carbon dioxide. If too much coal was extracted from the seam, the crushing weight of overhead rock forced down the roof and raised the floor of the gallery in 'the creep'.

Demand from London for coal rose steadily. In 1700 Newcastle was shipping 542,558 tons down the east coast. This had risen by 1732–3 to 729,394 tons. Daniel Defoe wrote:

> ... whereas when we are at London, and see the prodigious Fleets of Ships which come constantly in with coals for this increasing City, we are apt to wonder whence they come, and that they do not bring the whole Country away; so, on the contrary, when in this Country [Tyneside] we see the prodigious heaps, I might say Mountains, of Coals, which are dug up at every Pit, and how many of those Pits there are; we are filled with equal Wonder to consider where the People should live that can consume them.

The Newcomen engine, designed for the tin trade, was the first steam-powered device to be applied to coal-working. In 1715 the Liddells of Ravensworth, one of the biggest coal families, were negotiating for the supply of a steam engine capable of raising 10,000 gallons of water per hour from a depth of 150ft. This was intended for Gateshead Park colliery and apparently was still not delivered by 1722. By 1769 pumping engines were in general use—many from the designs of William Brown, 'viewer' or manager at Throckley colliery.

DEVELOPMENT OF LOCOMOTIVES

The next problem to be tackled was transport. The most westerly Tyne colliery was at Wylam, which was placed at a disadvantage by its distance from the staithes at Lemington. Benwell, which had installed a Brown pumping engine about 1762, laid down in 1797 a new kind of rail to convey coals to the staithe. This eliminated horse haulage by using a self-acting incline whereby the empty wagons were pulled up by the weight of full wagons descending. Horses formed no little part of the cost of transport and of haulage. As early as 1696, it was estimated that some 20,000 carriage and cart horses might be found between Newcastle and Sunderland, engaged in the coal trade. These horses could each consume in a year $1\frac{1}{2}$ tons of hay and 70 bushels of oats in addition to grass; they also required straw for bedding. By 1800 oats cost 2s a bushel.

Understandably, colliery owners were looking for a new form of traction, and gave every encouragement to their viewers, smiths and engineers to devise an engine to haul wagons. In 1812 Christopher Blackett's viewer, William Hedley, designed for Wylam colliery his own locomotive, which was built by Timothy Hackworth, the foreman blacksmith, and his staff, assisted by Thomas Waters, a Gateshead ironfounder. Because this first engine, made of cast-iron, was found defective, a second was designed of wrought-iron. This pulled, on trial, eight loaded wagons at the rate of four miles an hour, so vindicating Hedley's theory that smooth wheels could grip smooth rails. Hedley's engine, 'Puffing Billy', ran on the Wylam wagonway from 1813 to 1862.

Meanwhile at Coxlodge, north of Kenton, another system was being tried. The colliery, owned by the Brandling family, was about five miles from its staithes at Howdon. It had been opened only in 1807, and relied on cheap transportation. The Brandlings brought from their Leeds colliery the Blenkinsop engine, which moved on special rails furnished with pins into which cog-wheels on the engine engaged. Part of the Coxlodge line was built on this principle.

At West Moor and Killingworth the largest of the Tyne partnerships, nicknamed the 'Grand Allies', had opened another colliery in 1802 to work the High Main seam. It was their greatest achievement, in an association stretching back to 1725, when William Cotesworth of Gateshead had finally cajoled Henry Liddell of Ravensworth, George Bowes of Gibside, and Edward Wortley of Tanfield into agreement to limit production of coal from their collieries to maintain a reasonable price in London. In 1804 they engaged a new brakesman—the engineman attending to the winding gear. He came from one of the deepest of existing Tyne collieries, at Willington, and his name was George Stephenson. Stephenson was encouraged by the Killingworth viewer, Nicholas Wood, to study practical mechanics, and in 1812 was promoted to be enginewright. The following year Stephenson submitted his own proposals for a locomotive, which at its test on the Killingworth wagonway with its gauge of 4ft 8in drew the regulation eight loaded wagons (weighing 30 tons) up a gradient of 1 in 450 at 5 miles an hour. On 30 September 1816 George Stephenson and William Losh, a Walker ironfounder, patented a piston-driven locomotive. In 1821 Stephenson, backed by Nicholas Wood, persuaded Edward Pease of Darlington to include a locomotive among the forms of traction for his proposed horse-drawn tramway between Stockton and Darlington. In 1823 Stephenson and Pease went into partnership to manufacture these engines at Newcastle, a venture left largely to the direction of George's son, Robert Stephenson, a young man of twenty, schooled at Mr Bruce's Percy Street Academy, Newcastle, with a term at Edinburgh University.

The steam locomotive was now being offered not only as a local but also as a national form of transport for freight. Robert Stephenson's company supplied the rolling-stock for the Stockton and Darlington Railway. The Stephensons designed the *Lancashire Witch*, which was the first engine to have inclined cylinders and sprung axles, whereby the danger was reduced of the loco-motive shaking itself to pieces in motion. George's most famous engine was the *Rocket*, which in October 1829 won the Rainhill Locomotive Trials. This competition was a turning-point in loco-motive history, because it convinced waverers that under normal circumstances a moving engine was preferable to a succession of fixed haulage engines or a mixture of horses and self-acting inclined planes. The *Rocket*, with its multiple-tubed boiler, travelled faster and more economically than its rivals. The Stephensons now left Tyneside, to spread their railway systems over the world, but the Tyneside 'accent' went with them in the form of the gauge of the Killingworth wagonway on which the first engine-axles had been tested.

MINING HAZARDS

The early nineteenth century was of crucial importance for the Tyne coal trade. It saw the introduction of a new cheap transport, which enabled collieries at a distance from the river to offer com-petitive prices at the staithes. It also saw the end of many workings. The High Main seam had been exhausted, but improved pumping engines had enabled borings to be made to the Low Main seam, which was reached at Byker in 1800 at 792ft. This seam was reached at St Anthony's in 1805, but such was the honeycombing of the area that water soon seeped through from the Byker workings which had been abandoned because of the 'creep'. South of the Tyne, the Low Main seam had been reached at Hebburn in 1794, at Jarrow in 1803, and at Felling in 1810. There was a short period of overlap while both seams were being worked, then in 1811, because the High Main seam was exhausted, pumping

F

operations stopped at Felling. This had two devastating consequences. First, there was an explosion on 25 May 1812 in which ninety-two men and boys were killed. The disaster highlighted the urgent need for a safety-lamp for miners working in explosive atmosphere, and the Rev John Hodgson, rector of Jarrow, encouraged the formation of a society of colliery officers to consider measures for the prevention of mining accidents. Sir Humphrey Davy was invited to examine the problems involved, and in 1816 produced a lamp which protected its flame by a finely perforated shield through which the dreaded 'fire-damp' could not pass under normal conditions. George Stephenson invented a similar lamp which had some local popularity, and the 'Geordie' became synonymous with a Tyneside pitman. The second disastrous result of the stopping of the Felling pumps was a rise in water level throughout the Tyne basin. A pumping-station was kept in action at Friar's Goose at the expense of the owners of the Tyne Main, Felling, Walker, Wallsend, Willington and Heaton collieries, but this ceased working in 1851. It was hoped that 'tubbing' in the form of planks encasing the shafts where 'feeders' had been tapped, would be sufficient protection against the pressure of the water, but by 1857 the majority of the Tyne collieries had been flooded. Only the edges of the basin north and south of the Tyne could be worked with profit.

COMING OF THE RAILWAYS

In view of this flooding, the birth of the railway locomotive on Tyneside could be regarded in retrospect as a 'cuckoo in the nest'. It provided cheap transport for inland rivals at the moment of exhaustion of local supplies. There was, however, immediate rejoicing. Locomotive works were established, and the iron-works of Hawks, Crawshay at Gateshead and of Losh, Wilson and Bell at Walker were busy producing bars, cables and machine parts for locomotives as well as for pumping and stationary haulage engines. As early as 1825 Newcastle was planned as the terminus for a railway from Carlisle, bringing to an end the discussions started in 1794 about the desirability of a canal to connect the two towns and extend to the Solway for the export of Tyne coal to Ireland. The railway was estimated to cost £300,000 against the £355,067 for a canal. The line between Carlisle and Redheugh beside Gateshead was opened on 18 June 1838, and linked to Newcastle in 1839 by the Scotswood railway bridge. The same year of 1839 also saw the opening of the Newcastle and North Shields Railway. This latter line, with its great viaducts at Ouseburn and Willington Dene designed by John Green, was planned from the first as a passenger line, and is said to have carried in a week 51,252 passengers. Until 1845 the third- and fourth-class carriages had no doors and generally no roofs. In 1871 a branch line was added, to bring the workers to the gates of works and shipyards close to the river.

The need for a central railway junction in Newcastle became more urgent as plans ripened for the trunk line between Edinburgh and London, by the east coast route. Richard Grainger, the Newcastle speculative builder, visualised Elswick as the bridging-point over the Tyne and began property development in the Rye Hill area. He assumed that the level banks of the river would become factory sites, providing business for the railway—a prediction soon to be realised with the establishment by William G. Armstrong in 1847 of the Newcastle Cranage Company to build hydraulic machinery for cranes and dock-gates. Actually the Newcastle and Carlisle Railway Company acquired a more easterly site for their terminus by Forth Banks, outside the line of the town walls; and in conjunction with the York, Newcastle and Berwick Railway Company commissioned John Dobson, the foremost Newcastle architect of his day, to design a railway station. Despite modifications to accommodate railway offices, this building is one of Dobson's finest achievements, at once classical and contemporary. His use of curved iron ribbing to support a glass roof, itself curved to cover the sinuous platform necessitated by the cramped site, earned for Dobson the award of a gold medal at the Paris Exhibition of 1858 for novelty of design.

The Newcastle Central Station was opened by Queen Victoria on 29 August 1850. It was the culmination of engineering work started in 1846, which involved the bridging of the Tyne between the foot of West Street, Gateshead, and the castle at Newcastle at a level of 120ft above the river. The designer was Robert Stephenson. The total length of the bridge and its approaches was 1,370ft and it consisted of six spans of 125ft resting on coupled stone piers, themselves supported on timber piles embedded in the river. It was, incidentally, the first important bridge where the Nasmyth steam pile-driver was used. The ribs of the arches were of cast-iron forged at Gateshead. Above them were laid three sets of railway lines, supported by cast-iron pillars and cross-girders. Finally, in a true spirit of economy, a roadway was carried beneath the ribs on the stretchers which anchored the arches; and for the first time it was possible to cross from Gateshead to Newcastle at a high level.

REBUILDING OF CENTRAL NEWCASTLE

The construction of the High Level Bridge, completed in 1849, was the most momentous factor in the adaptation of Newcastle to the railway era. For centuries traffic had plunged down to the quayside and toiled up the opposite bank. Office development had stayed along the river-frontage, which also served the bridge traffic. Dean Street, built in 1784 over the Lort Burn, made a more civilised ascent to the castle plateau than the Side or Butcher Bank, and had been extended across Mosley Street as recently as 1839 by way of Grey Street to form a fashionable shopping centre. The *new* road-bridge leads directly past St Nicholas's church and the head of the Side into the Bigg Market, the ancient town thoroughfare. New office building followed. Dean Street and Pilgrim Street became backwaters. The Dobson and Grainger re-development of Newcastle's business centre was twisted westwards to emphasise Grainger Street, which was extended in 1868 to link with the Central Station and form one of the main shopping streets. New building took place on the roads giving access to the Central Station, including Westgate Road, which now was extended to meet the High Level Bridge. The connection of the Central Station to the main line to Berwick involved a mighty viaduct over the foot of Dean Street and the demolition of the ancient Barber-Surgeons' Hall in the Manors. It nearly involved the destruction of the old castle also, but the protests of outraged antiquaries prevailed. The railways, however, acted as a catalyst. The old business life, centred on the coal trade, stayed on the quayside. The new life of railways, shops and banking moved on to the plateau.

SHIPBUILDING

The bulk of Tyne coal continued to be sent to London by collier. These sturdy boats, slow but dependable, were built on Tyneside from Baltic timber, their sails made from Baltic flax, and their seams caulked with Baltic resin. The ship-yards lay on both sides of the Tyne from North and South Shields to Walker and Dunston. In general they were small businesses.

The challenge from inland rail-carried coal was taken up by Charles Mark Palmer, who with his brother George had started shipbuilding at Jarrow in 1852. The Palmers' first ship was the *John Bowes*, the first screw-propelled iron collier to be built on the Tyne. Charles Palmer had designed it to carry a load of 650 tons of coal to London in forty-eight hours, a service described as 'expeditious, regular and economical'. It was powered by engines capable of raising nine knots. The problem was to convince collier-owners that there were greater profits to be obtained from a £10,000 iron screw-collier than from a £1,000 sailing collier. This was effectively demonstrated by the *James Dixon*, which in 1863 delivered in London 62,842 tons of coal while manned by a crew of only twenty. Sixteen sailing colliers with 144 hands would have been required to deliver a similar quantity of coals.

Palmer's greatest innovation, however, was in the field of industrial organisation. He aimed to control the sources of supply for his yard and thereby eliminate middlemen's profits. To this end he had his own ironstone mine ten miles north of Whitby, his own port at nearby Mulgrave, where he shipped his ore in his own ships to his own furnaces and rolling-mills at Jarrow, to

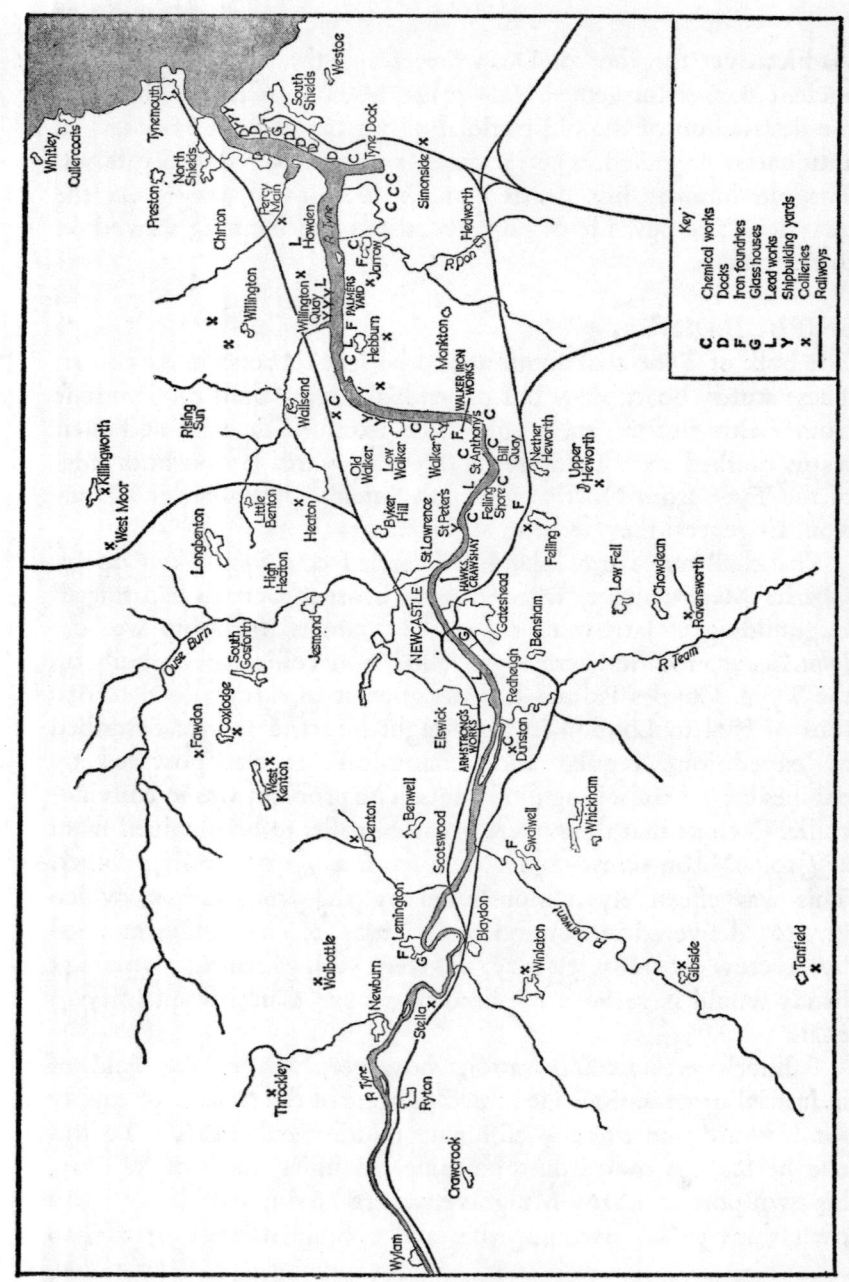

Fig 6 Industrial Tyneside about 1860

produce the iron used in his yards and engine-shops. The work force at Jarrow was approximately 3,500 men.

Palmer had taken advantage of the change from wooden to iron ships. Wooden ships were subject to the strains of heavy seas, but even more important, the weight of their own timbers meant a smaller hold than their water displacement would suggest. The pioneer of iron ships on Tyneside was J. H. S. Coutts. Coutts had been trained at Aberdeen and he established his yard at Low Walker in 1840. One of his first boats was the paddle-steamer, *Prince Albert*, which had plates of $\frac{3}{8}$ to $\frac{1}{4}$ in thickness. The iron ship plates, angles, bars and castings were supplied by the Walker Iron Works. More significant was his auxiliary screw collier, the *QED*. This ship of 271 tons was the first built to carry water as ballast in a double bottom. The introduction of water ballast was to have momentous consequences on Tyneside, because for centuries ships coming for coal had entered the river in ballast comprising such cheap, bulky commodities as scrap-iron, glass-sand and bricks. Many of the Tyne's subsidiary trades had been dependent for their materials on this ballast.

Shipbuilding, coal and railway locomotives were closely interlinked. The firm of R. & W. Hawthorn supplied the engines of the *QED*. Their original works had been founded in 1818 on the Forth Banks. Business, including locomotive building, enabled them to expand, until in 1871 they acquired the site of T. & W. Smith at St Peter's as an engineering works. In 1885 they amalgamated with the shipbuilding company of Andrew Leslie at Jarrow. Thereafter they established themselves as builders of oil tankers, Arctic exploration ships, troop-ships, ore carriers and other special service vessels. Equally enterprising was Charles Mitchell, who had followed Coutts from Aberdeen as his draughtsman. Having served with a London firm of marine engineers Mitchell set up in business for himself in Walker. He was a reasonable linguist and went to Europe for his orders. His *Hesperus* was built for Hamburg owners, although commandeered by the Admiralty in 1854 to carry iron rails for the Crimean War railway. In 1857 he built paddle-steamers for use on the Nile. More paddle-steamers were sent to Russia for use on the Volga and Caspian Sea, and to India for use on the Ganges. The years 1860 and 1861 saw two ocean-going steamers for Australia. Other orders included cable-laying steamers, a floating dock for the Dutch East Indies, three ice-breakers for Russia between 1895 and 1899, and four hydraulic suction dredgers for India and Australia in 1900. It was a far cry from the early days of wooden paddle-craft such as the *Tyne Steam Packet*, which began to ply from Newcastle to Shields in 1814, or the *Hylton Jolliffe*, which was the first to be put in regular summer service between the Tyne and London in 1827.

The search for new business led Charles Mitchell to supply frigates and turret-ships for the Russian and Chinese governments. In 1867 he began the fruitful connection with W. G. Armstrong for the supply of gun-boats to carry Elswick ordnance. From hydraulic machinery for cranes and dock-gates William Armstrong had moved into general engineering, until he was asked during the Crimean War to design submarine mines. Armstrong also let his imagination rove over field artillary, and designed a breech-loading rifled gun firing elongated lead missiles instead of cast-iron balls. This was officially reported to be fifty-seven times as accurate as ordinary artillery. As the British government was not prepared to back this innovation, Armstrong entered the international armaments market to recoup the expenses of development. Customers were found in Austria and Italy, Spain and Egypt, Denmark, Holland, Chile, Peru, and finally Russia. Because of the expertise of the Elswick works in hydraulic fittings, the furnishing of warships soon became a speciality. Hence the connection with Mitchell's yard at Walker. Their first joint ship was HMS *Staunch*. Over the next eighteen years about twenty similar ships were built—'floating gun carriages'. In 1884 the cruiser *Esmeralda* was built for the Chilean navy. It had a speed of 18 knots and incorporated the steel protective deck designed by George Rendel, a former manager of the Elswick Ordnance Works and since 1882 a Civil Lord of the Admiralty. By this date Sir William Armstrong had, in fact, absorbed the Low Walker yard into his armaments empire. His object was to rationalise his shipbuilding work by constructing his naval warships at Elswick, where the guns were made, and by transferring to Low Walker his civil orders for hydraulic dredgers and the like.

Meanwhile, increasing shipbuilding business in the 1870s had encouraged Mitchell to float a subsidiary company at St Peter's. This moved to a larger site in Wallsend after building its ninth ship, but soon fell into financial difficulties. A notable feature of the Tyne shipyards was, indeed, the brief duration of individual companies. Mitchell nominated his brother-in-law, C. S. Swan, as managing-director but Swan was killed in 1879 in a ferry accident, being struck by a paddle-steamer. His place was taken by George B. Hunter. There being a temporary boom in shipbuilding the company, now named Swan & Hunter, spread over an additional sixteen acres of land which had previously been occupied by Messrs J. & W. Allen, chemical manufacturers. Swan & Hunter was the first Tyne yard to build steel ships, in 1884–5. By 1903 it had absorbed the neighbouring companies of Wigham, Richardson of the Neptune Yard, Walker, and the Tyne Pontoons & Dry Docks Company of Wallsend. It now had a river frontage of nearly 1,400yd and an area of about 80 acres.

Mitchell had another protégé on Tyneside. In November 1871 he joined with the firms of Watts, Milburn of Blyth and Newcastle, and of Nelson, Donkin of North Shields and Newcastle to establish a repair-yard, the Wallsend Slipway. William Boyd, the second manager, was an enthusiast for marine engines and turned the attention of the slipway away from repairs to ships' hulls and towards the installation of ships' engines. In 1878 the company built the first steel boiler to be made on Tyneside—for the *Ethel*, which had been constructed at Mitchell's yard at Low Walker. In 1882 the company undertook to build the first triple-expansion engine on Tyneside. In 1905 it built its first steam turbine engines for SS *Immingham*, followed in 1906 by the great engines of the *Mauretania*, which herself was built by Messrs Swan, Hunter & Wigham, Richardson.

END OF THE IRON AGE

Railway competition killed the Tyne iron trade, because its one local resource was coal for smelting. Once the ironstone mines of Cleveland were opened up and provided by railway with South Durham coal at the Middlesbrough blast furnaces, the Tyneside foundries were unable to produce iron at a competitive price. Even their managers left for the new pastures. The manager of the Walker Iron Works, John Vaughan, left in 1840 to join in partnership with the businessman, Henry Bolchow, to found the first rolling mills and blast-furnaces at Middlesbrough. Isaac Lowthian Bell succeeded his father at Walker in 1845 as managing partner, where he installed new rail and plate mills, refineries, blast-furnaces and coke-ovens; but he left in 1850 to establish with his brother the Clarence Iron Works opposite Middlesbrough on the north bank of the Tees. The introduction of water ballast for Tyne colliers meant the end of cheap scrap iron. It was not enough to specialise in certain patented processes to retain customers. The last two foundries to survive were Hawks, Crawshay of Gateshead, which was finally auctioned in 1889, and the Walker Iron Works itself, which closed in 1891.

The railways brought a mobility of material and manpower which fractured irreparably the old industrial mould of supply first for local demand and for the greater world later. A speciality could now be delivered wherever there was a customer. Tyne locomotives and Tyne special-purpose ships could be sent all over the world; and the world's specialities could overwhelm local Tyneside trades such as glass-making, book illustration, or even iron-founding.

SELECT BIBLIOGRAPHY

J. BAILEY and G. CULLEY — *A General View of the Agriculture of Northumberland* (Newcastle, 1800)

G. C. GREENWELL — *A Glossary of Terms used in the Coal Trade* (1888)

E. HUGHES — 'The First Steam Engines in the Durham Coalfield' (*Arch Ael* 4th Series XXVII, 1949)

C. E. Lee	'The Wagonways of Tyneside' (*Arch Ael* 4th Series XXIX, 1951)
E. Mackenzie	*History of Northumberland* (Newcastle, 2nd ed, 1825)
W. Parson and W. White	*History, Directory and Gazetteer of Durham and Northumberland* (Newcastle, 1827)
L. T. C. Rolt	*George and Robert Stephenson* (1960)
L. Wilkes and G. Dodds	*Tyneside Classical* (1964)

Chapter 7

THE TECHNOLOGICAL
REVOLUTION

THOUGH technological experiments and dis-
coveries had encouraged a wider interest in pure science, English
institutions in the eighteenth and nineteenth centuries lagged
behind those of the continent. During this period, only Charles
Parsons could be matched by Britain against the many mechanical
pioneers of the continental universities and military schools: men
such as Sadi Carnot and Marc Brunel of France and the Siemens
brothers, N. A. Otto and Rudolf Diesel of Germany. The real
leaders of the sciences in Britain were the Scottish universities,
who produced technologists such as John Rennie. Tyneside's
contribution to scientific education at the beginning of the nineteenth century lay in the local schools and academies, where
mathematics, mechanics, navigation and book-keeping were
taught.

CHEMICAL TRADE
The production of salt from brine had started on Tyneside in
medieval times. The Leblanc process for making soda from common salt was brought to England about 1790. Seven years later
the earl of Dundonald had formed a partnership with John and
William Losh of Newcastle to exploit a patent of Dundonald for
the making of mineral alkali. When coal-boring at the Walker
colliery tapped a brine spring in the King Pit, the partners bargained with the colliery managers to have the brine pumped from
the pit to a new chemical works at Walker. An act of parliament
of 1798 specially exempted the Losh brothers from the salt tax,
provided that their brine was mixed with ground coke. This meant

that the salt was fit only for industrial use. The Losh Alkali Works soon changed from the Dundonald to the Leblanc process of soda-making. Such was the beginning of the Tyneside alkali trade, which supplied over half of the requirements for soda in England. Other chemical works on Tyneside followed, including Doubleday and Easterby, soap-boilers, at Bill Quay in 1800 and Messrs Cookson at Jarrow about 1823. By the mid-nineteenth century, Tyneside, with its vast coal resources for fuel, was supplying both soda and bleach for the English textile trade. Tennants, the Glasgow bleach manufacturers, moved to Tyneside about 1860.

Tyneside had more than coal to offer industrial chemists. Ferrous sulphate (copperas) was found naturally in the local coal-measures. After weathering from three to five years the copperas was roasted to produce sulphuric acid, required in the Leblanc process to decompose common salt. The resultant 'saltcake' when mixed with coal and limestone could be processed to form soda crystals or soda ash. The residue of the copperas was ground and mixed with other materials to form the colouring agents Venetian red or Prussian blue. Lead from Weardale and the Pennines was treated with hydrochloric acid (by-product of the Leblanc process) to make white and red lead for the paint trade. Hugh Lee Pattinson, a Tyneside metallurgical chemist of great distinction, patented in 1833 a method for the removal of silver from lead, based on the observation that lead crystallises whilst the silver is still molten. This enabled silver to be recovered from local lead at the rate of 300oz per ton; and his new process was soon in use throughout England and adopted by 1850 in France, Spain and Prussia. Pattinson had started at the soap factory of Anthony Clapham at Ouseburn, but transferred to become assayer of the Alston lead mines. In 1834 he founded the Felling Chemical Works with John Lee to manufacture soda, alum and Epsom salts.

Because of local complaints of air pollution, the chemical works were compelled to devise methods to recover their waste products; for it was estimated that the tall factory chimneys belched forth 12cwt of hydrogen chloride gas for every ton of salt decomposed, whilst a pall of calcium sulphide fumes hung over their waste tips. The most efficient firm in this direction was owned by Christian Allhusen, a German who invested in the declining alkali works of Charles Attwood at Gateshead. In 1841 he absorbed Doubleday and Easterby, the soap-boilers, and in the years thereafter built up a complex of plant serviced by wharves, steam cranes, an overhead railway, sidings and mechanical furnaces. Here nitre, chlorine and manganese were recovered. By 1891 pure sulphur derived from the Chance recovery process was being exported, a far cry from the time when a French monopoly of the Sicilian sulphur mines in the 1840s threatened, by a stoppage of supplies, to ruin the Tyne alkali trade.

TECHNICAL EDUCATION

Tyneside had more to offer even than raw material. It had the capital to attract men of ideas such as Archibald Cochrane, ninth earl of Dundonald. It commanded a large labour force. But as factories and processes grew in complexity it became all the more imperative that workers should have knowledge of the principles on which their work was based, and that scientifically minded manufacturers should have some forum for the interchange of ideas, to take advantage of each other's by-products.

The pioneer spirit in Newcastle was found in the Literary and Philosophical Society, established in 1793 as a debating society. In common with similar societies at Leeds, Birmingham, Sheffield and Manchester, the Newcastle society firstly enabled manufacturers to meet scientists, and secondly acted as sponsor for series of technical lectures. The principal speaker was the Rev William Turner, Unitarian minister of the Hanover Square Chapel, Newcastle, who was also the senior secretary of the Literary and Philosophical Society. The society owned a comprehensive library, to which women could have access as 'Reading Members'. At the opposite end of the social scale, a Mechanics' Institute was founded in Newcastle in 1824. Support came from local industrialists and coal-owners, and classes were provided in chemistry, mathematics, geography, architectural drawing and French. Members paid twelve shillings each year and the minimum age was twenty; young men were, however, admitted as reading members if they were over fourteen. By 1854, the library contained 10,000 books. Further mechanics' institutes were founded at Gateshead and Walker (1836), Wallsend (1850), Swalwell, Willington Quay and Howdon (1851). Employers regarded some technical education as desirable for their work-force, even if only to keep them off the streets and out of the beer-houses. The bulk of the institutes' funds derived from the workmen's fortnightly wages.

DURHAM COLLEGE OF MEDICINE

In 1831 Dr T. M. Greenhow, co-founder of the Newcastle Eye Infirmary in 1822, read a paper to the Literary and Philosophical Society. He proposed the establishment in Newcastle of an Academical Institution of the nature of a college or university for the promotion of literature and science, more especially amongst the middle classes of the community. The idea provoked considerable ridicule at the time, as local businessmen could see no profits from the joint-stock company which Dr Greenhow imagined would finance such a college.

Only the medical profession at that date could manifestly benefit by some scientific training. Many of the leading chemists of the eighteenth century—both inside and outside the universities —were medical practitioners; for in the words of Robert Bourne, reader in chemistry at Oxford University in 1797, a 'physician ignorant of chemistry cannot be well skilled in his profession'. A group of young doctors, therefore, headed by the brothers John and George Fife, leased premises in Bell's Court off Pilgrim Street, Newcastle, in 1832. Subjects offered for the benefit of local apprentices to the town's doctors included medicine, surgery and chemistry. Two years later they transferred to larger premises in the Barber-Surgeons' Hall in the Manors. The prospectus claimed that the school's lectures, demonstrations and dissections were recognised by the Royal College of Surgeons, London. Subsequently the school was re-constituted, and in 1852 it became affiliated to the recently established University of Durham (1835). Degrees of licenciate, bachelor and doctor in medicine were awarded. When the Barber-Surgeons' Hall was demolished in 1850–1 to make room for the railway viaduct, new premises were found in Westmorland House, adjoining the library of the Literary and Philosophical Society. Courses at the Durham College of Medicine could be attended singly, although there was a reduction of fees for quantity. Some students enrolled only for chemistry. Tuition here was provided by Dr Thomas Richardson, who had studied at Giessen in Germany under Professor Liebig. Richardson founded a superphosphate works at Blaydon and established an analytical laboratory in Portland Place, Newcastle.

MINING INSTITUTE

In 1852 the specialist needs of another professional group were satisfied by the establishment of the North of England Institute of Mining and Mechanical Engineers. Nicholas Wood, coal-owner and sometime viewer of Killingworth colliery, where he had encouraged George Stephenson whilst the latter was still the enginewright, had long argued the need for a recognised meeting-place for the exchange of knowledge and experimental demonstration. Once the Institute had been established on the site of Westmorland House, purchased from the College of Medicine, Nicholas Wood demanded the creation of a College of Mines. The council of the Institute supported his proposal, as there was no comparable school in the country (the Camborne School of Mines served the needs of the tin industry only). The duke of Northumberland, owner of the colliery at Percy Main, agreed to guarantee £10,000 towards the initial costs provided that a further £30,000 was found by other subscribers. It was also suggested that a coal royalty be levied throughout the country to provide the annual revenue. Tyneside, however, no longer represented the bulk of the coal trade, and the rest of the country was apathetic to the idea of a Mining College at Newcastle.

DURHAM COLLEGE OF SCIENCE

In 1868 the Newcastle Literary and Philosophical Society was addressed by Robert Spence Watson on the need to establish a university college, to teach all subjects except theology. There was a concurrent proposal to transfer to Newcastle the teaching of Durham University; and Lowthian Bell, formerly of the Walker Iron Works, urged the superiority of the railway facilities of Newcastle for student access. Other advantages were the existing collections of specimens held by the Natural History Society (1829), the presence of the College of Medicine, and a large local population of men who required technical instruction but not accommodation. This call for a university was answered on 11 March 1871, when a meeting was convened at the Literary and Philosophical Society under the chairmanship of Sir William Armstrong. Armstrong was the foremost industrialist of his day, not only on Tyneside but even in England, and his name was a guarantee of success. The subscription list was headed by Sir William with £600 and by Lowthian Bell with £300; and an appeal was launched for £30,000 as a permanent endowment.

Temporary accommodation for the college was found in the Coal Trade Chambers, and there was an initial enrolment in October 1871 of sixty-nine students, whose ages ranged from fifteen to forty-six. Of these, over half were under the age of eighteen. Thirty were registered as resident in Newcastle, thirteen as coming from Northumberland, twenty-one from County Durham, and one each from Carlisle, Huddersfield and Gloucester. It appears that no women had enrolled as day students before 1873, when classes in Greek were started. Seven ladies enrolled in 1871 for evening classes in geology or physics: amongst them was Miss Allhusen, almost certainly a relation of the Gateshead chemical manufacturer, who entered for chemistry, physics and geology.

The initial chairs were in mathematics, chemistry, experimental physics, and mineralogy with geology. The first professor of physics was A. S. Herschel, whose interest was electrical discharge and who helped Sir William Armstrong with experiments at the latter's home at Cragside, Rothbury, which was the second house in England to have electric lighting. The first professor of chemistry was A. Freire-Marreco, who was both a local consultant and reader in chemistry at the Durham College of Medicine. He continued

G

to hold both college appointments until his death in 1882. Thereafter the College of Medicine continued to utilise the chemistry teaching of the College of Science for its medical students, a practical collaboration which eventually led to the fusion of the two bodies in 1936 as King's College, Newcastle upon Tyne, in the University of Durham. In 1963 the University of Newcastle upon Tyne came finally into independent being.

The executive committee of the new College of Science, affiliated like Medicine to the nearby Durham University, contained many prominent local industrialists. Sir William Armstrong offered in 1874 a premium apprenticeship for the best student of the year; no mean award, as his Elswick engineering works was regarded as the best in the country. In 1880 the Durham Coal Owners' Association and the Steam Collieries Defence Association agreed to contribute to the salary of a professor of mining. Later a committee of the newly formed North East Coast Institute of Engineers and Shipbuilders under the presidency of William Doxford of Sunderland met to consider the provision of classes in mechanical, locomotive and marine engineering, shipbuilding and electrical engineering. In 1881 R. L. Weighton was appointed from the drawing-office of Messrs Wigham, Richardson of Wallsend to be professor of engineering at a minimum salary of £500 a year. This professorship was one of the most valuable appointments in the college at that date. The king of the Belgians agreed to subscribe £500 to the 'Stephenson Engineering Department'. Further financial aid came from the Treasury. There was also a proposal, realised in 1891, to establish a new faculty of agriculture to provide rural lecturers and run experimental farms to study artificial manures, grass-seeds and dairying.

TECHNICAL COLLEGES

Other institutions, however, were emerging on Tyneside for technical education. At South Shields there was the Marine School, founded within the Mechanics' Institute in 1861, for the instruction of seamen and sea-going engineers and for the training of shipmasters and officers. By 1888 exhibitioners from the Marine

School were seeking admission to the Durham College of Science. The Bath Lane Schools had been established in Newcastle in 1878 by the Newcastle School Board at the instigation of J. H. Rutherford, doctor and nonconformist preacher, with the object of preparing students for the examinations of the Department of Science and Art at Kensington. Following the death of Dr Rutherford in 1890, the newly built technical school in Bath Lane, replacing inadequate premises, was named the Rutherford Memorial College. In 1897 objections were lodged by Newcastle ratepayers that their technical education rate was supporting two institutions, Rutherford College and the Durham College of Science, whose work was virtually identical.

In fact, according to the report of an investigating committee, the bulk of the Rutherford students were under the age of eighteen, whilst the age of admission to the College of Science had been raised in May 1896 from sixteen to eighteen. Overlapping occurred mainly in the field of evening-work, where both offered to apprentices courses in natural science, mechanics, mining, agriculture, hygiene (for plumbers), physiography and navigation. Not until 1909 was it agreed that Rutherford College should be solely responsible for teaching elementary or predominantly technical subjects, such as building-construction, plumbing, telegraphy and typography, whilst the College of Science undertook all work of advanced standard, as costly equipment might be involved. This applied especially to electrical and marine engineering. Rutherford College of Technology is now part of Newcastle Polytechnic, established in 1969, and one of the largest such institutions in England.

The cause of technical education, however, was by no means won. Despite lip-service, industrialists preferred 'practical men'. Only in 1897 could the College of Science convince the Board of Examiners that it could prepare students for the Colliery Managers' Certificate. Conservatism was perhaps less entrenched in electrical engineering, and Dr W. M. Thornton was appointed lecturer and later professor in the subject. His personal contributions to local industry were improvements in mine-lighting and machinery.

In 1905 an appeal was made to local shipbuilders and ship-owners to endow a school of naval architecture, a subject studied elsewhere at an advanced level only at the universities of Glasgow and Liverpool and at the Royal Naval College, Greenwich. In consequence, in December 1906, J. J. Welsh of Messrs Laird Brothers, Birkenhead, was appointed the first professor of naval architecture at Newcastle, at the then enormous salary of £1,100 a year. But the students were middle-class young men with no previous connection with shipping, and only reinforced the suspicions of employers and workers alike.

STEAM TURBINES

The university-trained engineer was regarded as a freak. He could, however, be wildly successful, if he had sufficient backing. Charles A. Parsons, the son of an Irish peer, had studied mathematics at Cambridge, and whilst still an undergraduate at St John's College he patented in 1876 his version of an epicycloidal engine, the forerunner of his steam turbine. He was placed eleventh wrangler in 1877, and immediately entered Armstrong's works at Elswick as a premium apprentice to gain practical engineering experience. Subsequently he joined the engineering firm of Clarke, Chapman of Gateshead, where he developed a steam turbine to generate electricity. In 1889 Parsons left Gateshead to establish his own works at Heaton for making his marine steam turbine. The first ship to be fitted with this engine was the *Turbinia*. She stunned the world of marine engineering in June 1897 by circling the warships at the Jubilee Naval Review off Spithead at 34½ knots, a speed never before attained on water.

The engineering world, however, still pinned its faith to triple- and quadruple-expansion engines. The marine turbine was economical only at high speeds, and such were required only by gunboats or perhaps cross-channel ferries. Its use by large liners was not contemplated until competition from German merchant shipping on the Atlantic crossing provoked the British government to offer an annual subsidy of £150,000 to the Cunard Company, provided it placed orders for two steamships 'capable of maintaining during a voyage across the Atlantic a minimum average speed of from 24 to 25 knots in moderate weather'. As the ships were to be regarded as auxiliary cruisers, a Treasury loan of £2,600,000 was made available for their construction. For the engine the committee chose Parsons's turbine, which represented 70,000 horse-power. The ships' hulls for the *Lusitania* and *Mauretania* were ordered on Clydeside and Tyneside respectively. Thereafter other passenger lines adopted the turbine engine where speed was a consideration.

OIL TANKERS

Parsons's turbine was powered by steam-coal, and it needed more than a hundred firemen to stoke the boilers of the *Mauretania*. Meanwhile other sources of energy were under consideration. Oil had been used as a fuel for marine boilers as early as 1859, but its main development must be associated with the German Rudolf Diesel. Tyneside concentrated on developments to the tanker's hull rather than its engines. The first British oil tankers, the *Atlantic* and the *Great Western*, were built in the 1860s by Rogerson & Company of Byker. They were themselves sailing ships designed to carry oil, although there is no evidence that they ever carried anything but general cargo. From 1872 Palmers of Jarrow launched a series of oil-carriers incorporating the tanks in the ship's fabric. The final stage of development was reached in 1886 with the *Loutch* and the *Gluckauf*, built by Hawthorn, Leslie of Hebburn and by Armstrong, Mitchell of Walker respectively. These identified the outer shell of the ship with the skin of the tank, the concept of the modern tanker. Tyneside maintained its world position as leading builder of oil tankers until 1913.

ELECTRICITY

The other great source of power was electricity. Whilst at Clarke, Chapmans of Gateshead, Charles Parsons had been head of the electrical department, manufacturing small turbo-dynamos for lighting installations on ships. From this he developed a condensing turbine for land-based electric supply companies, his first order being in 1891 for a unit of 100kW capacity for the Cambridge Electric Light Station. By 1900 the Parsons works at Heaton was building turbo-alternators of 1,250kW capacity; and in 1914 the Carville Power Station at Wallsend, owned by the Newcastle upon Tyne Electric Supply Company, was equipped with turbo-alternators of 11,000kW capacity, running at 2,400rpm—the first large high-speed sets in the world.

This demand for electrical power came indirectly from the researches of a Gateshead chemist, Joseph Wilson Swan. Swan had trained as a pharmacist, and in 1846 joined John Mawson in a pharmacy business in Mosley Street, Newcastle. Here he dabbled in photography and developed a process for the manufacture of collodion. In 1864 Swan patented a carbon process for photographic printing. At the same time he was experimenting with carbonised paper to act as a filament to conduct electric current in a vacuum. Following the development of the mercury vacuum pump, Swan resumed work on his incandescent lamp, and made a preliminary demonstration of it in December 1878 before the Newcastle upon Tyne Chemical Society. He refined the composition of the filament, trying a plastic substance, formed from nitrocellulose dissolved in acetic acid, extruded as fine threads from metal dies under pressure. This process, patented in 1883, not only revolutionised the manufacture of carbon filament lamps but was also an early step in the evolution of artificial silk. Swan also worked on the problem of electric batteries to supply the current for his lamps; and in 1881 invented the cellular lead plate, which greatly enlarged the storage-capacity of a given size of cell. Such batteries were less clumsy than the prototype accumulator batteries of the Frenchmen R. L. G. Planté and C. Faure, and were widely used in the early direct-current generating-stations.

In 1880 Swan had formed, with the support of Sir William Armstrong, Robert Spence Watson and Dr J. T. Merz, a company for production of his lamps at South Benwell. The lamps were sold according to their working voltage and approximate candle-power, each one being tested individually. Initially used for house lighting, the electric lamp was quickly adapted for lighting shops, the House of Commons (1881), trains and theatres. Despite high costs of production, orders for lamps streamed into Swan's factory, including an American order for 25,000 lamps to be despatched within a fortnight. This brought patent difficulties because, whilst Swan regarded his researches as merely a link in the chain of electrical improvements, Thomas A. Edison in America had taken out five English patents covering incandescent lamps. In 1882 Edison sued Swan's company for infringement, and after litigation it was agreed to merge interests by founding the Edison & Swan United Electric Light Company in October 1883, with an authorised capital of £1,000,000. This spelt the departure from Tyneside of the lamp factory to London, although at the Lemington Glassworks, eventually acquired by the General Electric Company, bulbs, including television tubes, continued to be blown until the 1960s.

The first Newcastle street lighting by electricity was outside Swan's shop in Mosley Street. In 1889 Dr Theodore Merz, Robert Spence Watson and J. T. Gibson formed the Newcastle Electric Supply Company, which accepted responsibility for lighting the east of the town. This company was the main customer for the Parsons generators. Recognition that gas was obsolescent as a form of illumination came when in 1900 the Walker and Wallsend Union Gas Company secured an act of parliament to enable it to supply industry in Wallsend, Howdon and Willington with electricity. The gas company already possessed the site for their proposed power-station at Neptune Bank in Wallsend. To forestall a possible rival the Newcastle Electric Supply Company offered to supply electricity in bulk to the gas company.

The Newcastle Electric Supply Company, which already had the monopoly of lighting east Newcastle, now hoped to supply power to Tyneside. In 1902 it obtained the contract to supply the coal mines north of Wallsend, and in 1903 it was authorised by act of parliament to supply the North Eastern Railway Company with electricity. The following year the loop railway from Newcastle to Tynemouth and Whitley Bay was electrified, being the first outside London. At this stage the Newcastle Electric Supply

Company was supplying electricity to an area of about 600 square miles on both sides of the Tyne and a new power-station was required. Carville, built on the site of a disused Wallsend chemical works, was operating by June 1904, and was the largest generating station in Great Britain. The nearby shipyards and factories discarded their own generating plant and took their supplies from the company. Collieries took to electrically-driven coal-cutters and conveyers, as well as electric lighting. A number of firms introduced electric furnaces for their smelting operations.

Other ideas for harnessing electricity were developed by J. H. Holmes of Newcastle, who specialised in the manufacture of small dynamos, train lighting sets, electric drive for printing presses, and the portable lighting sets used on the Suez Canal for night navigation. Meanwhile, across the river at Hebburn, Messrs A. Reyrolle, who had transferred their business from London in 1901, were building switch-gear for power-stations, to reap the advantages of a local market of great potential.

Cheap electric power gave a fillip on Tyneside to the declining chemical industry. Experimental work by the Solvays in Belgium had produced a new method for the manufacture of soda which was cheaper than the Leblanc process and did not bring in its wake the devastating by-products of hydrogen chloride and calcium sulphide, or overproduction of bleach and caustic soda. The new safety regulations after 1878 and the expense of recovery plant hit the Leblanc soda-makers. To rationalise the trade, these formed an alliance, whereby the twenty-four chemical works on Tyneside were reduced to four; but by the turn of the century it was decided to abandon the Leblanc process and exploit the salt beds at Billingham on Tees. The Solvay process did not require coal to evaporate the brine. The United Alkali Company, however, continued to use the efficient Allhusen works at Gateshead to produce caustic soda by electrolysis. Tankloads of brine were delivered from Billingham to take advantage of cheap Tyneside electricity. As late as 1911, the census returns listed 1,033 chemical workers in Gateshead, the largest group of such workers in County Durham. North of the Tyne, the Castner Kellner Alkali Company transferred its sodium department from Runcorn to Wallsend in 1906, to benefit from the cheap electricity.

Tyneside electricity also attracted to Wallsend the Thermal Syndicate Ltd. This company manufactured electrical insulators and vessels for the chemical trade, its material being fused silica. This has special properties of resistance to sudden changes in temperature, and melts at about 1,750°C. The initial research was done by staff from the firm of Merz, McLellan, consulting engineers to the Newcastle Electric Supply Company, and power was obtained from the Neptune Bank generator. By 1906 production began on a commercial scale.

During the technological advances of the nineteenth century Tyneside was a centre of great importance, developing new industries at a time when the export of coal was no longer sufficient to provide employment for a growing population.

SELECT BIBLIOGRAPHY

R. APPLEYARD   *Charles Parsons, his life and work* (1933)

G. BLAKE   *Lloyd's Register of Shipping 1760–1960* (Lloyd's Register, 1960)

W. A. CAMPBELL   *A Century of Chemistry on Tyneside 1868–1968* (Soc of Chemical Industry, 1968)
The Chemical Industry (1971)

D. EMBLETON   *The History of the Medical School: afterwards the Durham College of Medicine at Newcastle . . . 1832 to 1872* (Newcastle, 1890)

A. E. MUSSON and ERIC ROBINSON   *Science and Technology in the Industrial Revolution* (Manchester, 1969)

C. SINGER (ed)   *A History of Technology* (Oxford, 1958) vols iv and v

Chapter 8   LIVING CONDITIONS ON
                  TYNESIDE, 1830–1910

IN the first quarter of the nineteenth century, Tyneside moved into its era of technical expansion. We must now consider how the workers lived, organised themselves to improve their conditions of labour, and took their leisure.

PUBLIC HEALTH
The precise conditions under which the workers lived were virtually unknown, except to those whose business required personal contact, such as the doctor or man of religion. Even here the worker was encouraged to make the necessary approaches through the local dispensary or class-meeting. This ignorance was shattered with the onset of cholera on Tyneside in 1831. The first English casualties in this epidemic, which had swept Europe, occurred at Sunderland in October 1831. There the sickness was contained until 7 December, when it broke out in Newcastle. Property-owners were exhorted to have the interiors of their tenements washed with hot lime, and emergency hospitals were opened in each parish of the town. Out of 971 persons infected, 306 died. In North Shields the outbreak began on 10 December, and out of 258 cases, 91 died. As it spread to Gateshead and Newburn, the story was the same. While physicians argued as to the causes and treatment of the disease there was an outcry that over-crowded houses, in disorganised juxtaposition, provided a disease-ridden canker in the heart of cities from which even the wealthy might receive infection. A theory that epidemics were carried by a 'miasma' or vapour that settled over the stricken community encouraged sanitary reformers to insist on through-draughts for

streets and open windows for houses to disperse the foul air. They were met by almost insurmountable obstacles. Municipal corporations had no power to insist that building contractors lay sewers, pave streets, or even build in methodical rows. Nor could they levy rates to provide these facilities themselves. A public campaign had to be waged to heighten awareness of the general danger to health lurking in town slums. In 1842 the Poor Law Commissioners instituted an inquiry throughout England and Wales into the causes of death among the destitute, which developed into the Health of Towns Commission. This reported in 1845 on paving, cleansing, drainage, sewerage, ventilation, water supplies, and dwelling and lodging houses. The Tyneside inquiry was undertaken by Dr D. B. Reid.

One of the outstanding nuisances was the accumulation of middens in the streets, alleys and courts. While the principal streets of Newcastle were swept by scavengers from two to six times a week, courts and alleys not used as thoroughfares were the responsibility of none to clean. Poor families, unprovided with any sanitary conveniences, either put out their night-soil with any other refuse for the scavenger to collect each morning or dumped it in lanes and vacant plots under cover of night. In Pipewellgate, Gateshead, there were 2,040 inhabitants and only three privies. In South Shields, however, there was a daily collection of refuse and night-soil. In the course of a later report on conditions in North Shields, in 1851, Mr Mitchell, superintendant of police, described courts where 'the stairs leading to the court are covered with offal and refuse matter... In the centre of the court there is a dunghill, containing ... about 20 loads of manure and refuse matter... There is no privy accommodation.' Because the Tyneside street-middens provided agricultural manure, they were regarded as a source of profit.

The sanitary problem was compounded by overcrowding. Large houses in the Close, Sandhill and Quayside at Newcastle, or in Church Street and Pipewellgate in Gateshead, once the homes of wealthy merchants, had on their departure to residential suburbs, been sublet as tenements with one family to a room. The height of the rooms varied from six to eight feet and some contained as many as ten people. There was generally but one window to a room, and that not made to open. Few houses had water laid on, and the inhabitants had to queue at the nearest stand-pipe or wait on the water-cart; those living upstairs had the toil of carrying pails up and then down, 'which operates much against the cleanliness and comfort both of their habitations and persons'. Mr Mackinley, surgeon, referring to North Shields in 1851, gave as his opinion that the weekly wash, 'done in the same room in which the family eat and sleep', by saturating the air with steam was a positive cause of the high mortality in the town. The census of 1851 paid special attention to this question of overcrowding and the multiple occupation of houses; and Gateshead provides some choice examples. In Church Street the 14 tall eighteenth-century houses contained 51 households, totalling 228 persons. One tenement housed no less than 51 people.

The base of this pyramid of squalor was to be found in the common lodging-houses. The homes of 'vagrants, trampers, and all those who have no fixed habitation or employment', they were recognised as hot-beds of infectious disease. In Newcastle in 1845 there were sixty-three such establishments, generally situated in the narrowest of lanes, sleeping two lodgers to a room. Conditions in Gateshead and North Shields were discreetly overlooked by Dr Reid, but in 1849 official wrath in Gateshead denounced the twenty-six lodging-houses of Pipewellgate as 'disgusting dormitories'. Here 395 persons were crowded into seventy-four rooms, without regard to age, sex or sickness. The wretched lodgers are described as 'thieves, mariners, widows with large families, and writers of begging-letters'. Confirmatory evidence of these denunciations is provided by the 1851 census returns.

As for North Shields, the lodgings-houses reported upon in 1851 were grim, the beds accommodating three people each. In one such 'doss-house' on Steam-mill Bank the police found during a raid:

> . . . 11 persons who had been living for a considerable period of time on no other visible means than that of pilfering. . . They were regaling

themselves with a piece of roast beef, eggs, tea, and some hot whisky toddy. The apartments of the house were in the most filthy condition that could be imagined; it beggars description. In one of the cupboards, having occasion to search for some stolen property, there was a deposit of human filth; there were four beds in the room, three persons to a bed; behind the beds was a hen-roast, with a deposit of filth; the effluvium from the room was most overpowering. Connecting that apartment with the room above was a trap-door, by which a person could escape from one apartment to another when pursued by the police. . .

There was a pathetic belief that the natural steepness of the ground reduced the need for systematic drainage. This was little comfort to folk living in the streets running along the river banks, which often lacked paving and received 'the accumulated liquid refuse discharged from the steep banks'. Gateshead's public sewers, all 1,000 yards of them, had no means by which they could be cleaned. The river provided 'the only trustworthy source of supply of water for the great bulk of the inhabitants', although Dr Reid's investigating committee hopefully suggested that they might make better use of rain-water by providing each house with a large tank. Some houses had private wells.

The publication of the report of the Health Commission coincided with agitation over the repeal of the Corn Laws. Not until a second cholera epidemic swept England in 1848–9 were reformers able to pass the Public Health Act of 1848. This created a central board of health with powers to authorise local boards where the death rate was above 23 per 1,000 or where 10 per cent of the district's inhabitants wanted such a board. A direct result of this act was the Tynemouth inquiry of 1851, to enable the new corporation to assume powers to carry drains and sewers through private property, pave and control the lay-out of new streets, provide public conveniences and wash-houses, control slaughter-houses, and organise an adequate supply of water. None of these powers had been given to Tynemouth on its incorporation in 1849, nor could it levy special rates for such purposes. These local boards to regulate sanitary conditions were to provide an embryo of local government, adding a measure of representative control over local amenities.

POOR LAW

Public health reform grew from a concern with the condition of the poor because poverty led to malnutrition and susceptibility to disease. Humanitarianism, however, was not the only driving force. There was also a desire to economise in wasted life. Yet before repeating the charges against the Poor Law Commissioners of 1834 and their unsparing secretary, Edwin Chadwick, it is well to be reminded that on Tyneside at least the new Poor Law was put into operation with flexibility and common sense. Tyneside had escaped the period of depression in the mid 1830s which brought hardship to the textile trades, and there were no masses of unemployed to be found accommodation in 'repellent' workhouses. Previously care of the poor had been the responsibility of the parish, and Mackenzie in 1827 spoke harshly of the St Nicholas's Poor House, where 'the sick and the healthy are necessarily huddled together into small rooms, in each of which two or three beds are usually occupied by the diseased and dying'. Their diet consisted of broth and bread, with boiled meat twice a week, and it was estimated that their keep cost 3s 9½d a week. The causes were a reluctance of the select vestry and 'respectable parishioners' to levy and pay an adequate poor rate, and bad management. St John's Poor House was able to provide meat five days a week at a cost of 3s 1d, and reaped its reward in a healthy community of inmates.

The new system of Poor Law Unions replaced the parish with a regional grouping. Tyneside unions north of the river consisted of Castle Ward, which included Newburn; Newcastle and its suburbs; and Tynemouth, which extended as far north as Blyth, and covered Wallsend and Longbenton. South of the river were the unions of South Shields, stretching from Whitburn to Jarrow, and of Gateshead, stretching from Heworth to Whickham and Ryton. Substantial workhouses to accommodate these enlarged populations for which the 'guardians' were responsible were built at Tynemouth, Ponteland, Gateshead, South Shields, and on Westgate Road, Newcastle. The pooling of resources appears to have enabled the local guardians to improve conditions of both in-door and out-door relief. When it was shown to the Poor Law Commissioners that the working classes on Tyneside fed better than in some other northern districts, approval was given for a more generous allowance of food in local workhouses.

The role of the guardians of the poor was to provide relief for the destitute, for the deserving poor; but what of the profligates and those unemployed on account of strikes? Between August and October 1815 there had been a seamen's strike on Tyneside over redundancy arising from the end of the Napoleonic Wars and a run-down of the navy. The shipowners agreed to pay a minimum of £3 a voyage to London but refused to accept a quota of men based on the tonnage of the ship. Local popular sympathy was with the seamen, and the magistrates showed great reluctance to coerce the men to return to work by calling upon the militia. Another strike was called over wages in 1825, shortly after the establishment in South Shields of the Seamen's Loyal Standard Association. This was a benefit society, designed to help seamen and their families 'in case of shipwreck, sickness, superannuation and death', and its articles of association expressly denied financial assistance to strike-picketers: but John Harrison, a committee member, was convicted for his part in the 1825 strike in intimidating non-member seamen from putting to sea.

EARLY TRADE UNIONS

The keelmen had established a benevolent society as early as 1701, and there were major strikes in 1809, 1819 and 1822 to raise their wages and maintain the level of work available following the increased use by coal-shippers of mechanical spouts to load the keels. The keelmen's resistance was fed by various friendly societies; and it is interesting to find that their employers in 1819 made a contribution of £300 to clear the debts of the keelmen's charity.

The pitmen formed their first trade union in 1825, following the repeal of the Combination Acts. This was the United Association of Northumberland and Durham Miners, and may have had some co-operative undertones. After what proved a false start a new union was formed in 1830, largely as the result of work by Thomas Hepburn. When the time approached in March 1831 for the renewal of the annual bond or working agreement between pitman and colliery-owner, meetings of pitmen were held outside Gateshead and on the Newcastle Town Moor, when the men were urged to demand regular work and wages, and shorter hours for boys working underground. The mayor of Newcastle, Archibald Reed, was invited to act as mediator. The employers stood firm, regarding a possible stoppage as a convenient excuse to raise London coal prices; and by April the pitmen tightened their pressure by forcing such collieries as were still working to join the strike.

After seven weeks the coal-owners agreed to a 10 per cent increase in wages and the restriction of working hours for boys to twelve hours a day.

In the following spring the pitmen tried the same tactics. The coal-owners brought in outside labour and evicted their workers from their tied cottages. Violence increased, with the murder in June 1832 of Nicholas Fairles, a South Shields magistrate who had been attempting to organise the militia to guard Jarrow Colliery. Finally, in August, the pitmen agreed to return to work in the face of permanent loss of employment by the substitution of outside labour from as far afield as Cornwall and Ireland. The union was broken financially, having attempted to pay 6s a week to strikers. Thomas Hepburn was given the choice of renouncing union activities or being debarred from any gainful employment. He chose the former.

Unrest in the coal-mines had been nationwide during 1831 and 1832. In 1841 the miners of the West Riding of Yorkshire proposed a Miners' Association of Great Britain and Ireland, with the aim of standardising hours of labour and maximising wages; a fund was to be raised to provide legal aid for miners prosecuted for breach of contract of employment. In 1843 the headquarters of the association was established at Newcastle. A specimen bond was produced, to last for six months only, which guaranteed a four-day week and offered a ten-hour day. The owners denied that the association had any authority over its members and refused to negotiate. The nationwide strike collapsed, but on 5 April 1844 the pitmen of Northumberland and Durham withdrew their labour. Although the central government discouraged the use of military force to protect the collieries the owners employed their own stalwarts, who evicted recalcitrant pitmen from their cottages and installed outside labour, attracted by the comparatively high wages. Public sympathy was again on the side of the pitmen, more especially with the hardship inflicted on their families at the time of eviction, but it had no tangible expression in money and the men returned to work on a monthly basis, a change earlier rejected because it lacked the security of the yearly bond. A depression in the coal trade between 1847 and 1848 completed the extinction of this union.

Working-men's associations had a dual purpose—to improve wages and labour conditions and to provide some security for the sick, aged and dependents. In 1864 Thomas Burt helped to form the Northumberland Miners' Mutual Confident Association, soundly based on high subscriptions and dedicated to win the coal-owners' confidence by its reluctance to strike and its control over its membership. This policy bore fruit in December 1871, when the Northumberland Miners held their first joint conference with the Northumberland Coal Owners Association.

In the Tyneside coal mines by the 1860s a two-shift system of work was employed underground, each pitman working about seven hours a day. The boys leading the corves or working the ventilation doors worked the double shift of between twelve to thirteen hours. In the ship-yards the shipwrights had secured a fifty-seven-hour week. In engineering, where the growth of the great industrial complexes of Armstrong and of Hawthorn meant an increasing demand for labour, there was pressure from the men for a nine-hour working day, while the managements were more interested in piece-rates which reduced the costs of supervision. The argument for reduced hours was that it would produce a more alert labour-force, which could use the increased leisure constructively by attending night-school and improving its technical knowledge, instead of tumbling exhausted into the nearest public house before rolling home drunk, to sleep. (In its heyday Scotswood Road, in which Armstrong's works were situated, boasted over a hundred public houses and beershops sporting such names as the Hydraulic Crane, Ordnance, Gun, Rifle and Vulcan).

The image of Tyneside as the home of heavy industry was imprinted on national awareness by the great strike of 1871 which paralysed the engineering works of Armstrong, Hawthorn, W. Abbott of Gateshead, and all their Tyneside associates, with the important exceptions of Palmers of Jarrow, the shipbuilders, and R. Stephenson the locomotive builders.

After a brief strike in the spring of 1871, the engineering employers on Wearside had granted their men a reduction of their working day to nine hours. In April 1871 representatives of the various Tyneside works similarly engaged met to establish a Nine Hours' League with the object of negotiating on this point with their own employers. The movement was emphatically not inspired by the Amalgamated Society of Engineers, founded in 1851, which viewed the impending conflict with dismay: the league was organised by an ad hoc committee. On 22 May, having failed to persuade their employers to meet them to discuss terms, this committee recommended their fellows to hand in their notice and some 7,500 men began their twenty-week strike. One of the first moves of the employers was to persuade local millers and flour merchants to refuse credit to strikers and their families; this ban, however, was made less effective by the growth of retail food shops throughout the area. This was followed by a call for an 'anti-strike' fund from employers outside Tyneside, whose notable lack of co-operation included the willing employment of Tyneside skilled workers. On 3 August, the employers offered as a compromise a fifty-seven hours' basic week, similar to that enjoyed on Clydeside, but the Nine Hour's League refused to be deflected from its demand. The employers thereupon recruited more than a thousand foreign workmen from Belgium, Germany,

Denmark, Norway and Sweden. This provoked a violent reaction both locally and from the Amalgamated Society of Engineers; and the police courts were kept busy prosecuting those who molested these foreign workers.

The strikers were particularly well led by men with moderate views and considerable organising ability. Of prime importance were popular sympathy and its expression in financial support. Contributions to the strike fund were received from the engineers at the Gateshead depot of the North Eastern Railway and at Stephensons, who continued to work on the understanding that should the other Tyneside employers grant the nine-hour day they should benefit similarly. Distribution was on a works basis to enable special cases of hardship to be taken into consideration. The Northumberland Miners' Association began to contribute £20 a week, raised subsequently to £40 a week. Joseph Cowen, a known radical and owner-editor of the *Newcastle Chronicle*, gave the fund his personal guarantee and encouraged donations from like-minded industrialists. By 20 June there was strike-pay of 3s a week, with an additional 6d for each dependent child. By the end of the strike on 7 October 1871, the organisers had raised and disbursed over £20,000.

The Tyneside employers had been stiffened in their resistance to their men's demands by the indignation of Sir William Armstrong, who regarded Elswick as his private estate. This paternalistic attitude was shared by Sir Charles Mark Palmer, who when faced in 1866 by his men at Jarrow with a demand for a nine-hour day had harangued them on the dangers of foreign competition and threatened them with a lock-out. In 1871 Palmer again met his men, but this time offered to give them the benefits of the nine-hour day when locally agreed, provided that they remained at work during the current strike. The owners of the other firms lacked such traditions of joint development, and here the *business* consequences of meeting the men's demands for a shorter week, which was the equivalent to a rise in wages, were paramount. Their resolution was weakened only when faced with the complete loss of the skilled labour of their men as they found employment elsewhere in the country, where wages were between 6s and 12s a week higher. Furthermore, they were losing orders to other regions. In September the league's leader, John Burnett, declared that the men wanted a shorter working-week, not higher wages. If the employers would yield to fifty-four hours a week the workers would accept a proportionate drop in wages. The employers knew, however, as well as the workers that skilled men cost money, and that the fall in wages was impracticable. Finally, a compromise was reached whereby the men had a recognised fifty-four-hour week, but would work such overtime as the employers required. The wage rates would remain as they had been before the strike. By 12 October 1871 most of the men were back at work, after a most successful local non-union strike.

OCCUPATIONS ON TYNESIDE
The census returns of 1871 show that Newcastle and Gateshead housed 3,754 engineers and 2,574 iron-workers. Despite popular belief, however, heavy industry was not the only occupation on Tyneside. Already there was a considerable 'service industry'— exclusive of the labour of over 7,000 domestic servants in Newcastle alone. The census returns of 1871 enumerate for Newcastle 192 police officers, 115 schoolmasters and 207 schoolmistresses, 957 tailors, 1,224 shoemakers, 90 hairdressers, 114 hatters, 615 commercial clerks, 738 masons and paviors, 210 plasterers, 411 butchers and 473 grocers, 51 booksellers, 64 solicitors and 72 law clerks, 95 surgeons and 147 druggists. The Trade Directories provide a hint of the introduction of such novelties as fishmongers (1844), instead of the street hawkers or market stallholders, greengrocers (1844), boot and shoe shops (1851), outfitters (1851), piano dealers (1861) and wine and spirit merchants (1861). The coast railway enabled Newcastle businessmen to have their homes at Tynemouth or Cullercoats, to enjoy the benefits of salt-water bathing tapped to their own houses. Whitley Bay could develop as a holiday resort.

Incomes on Tyneside ranged from those of Sir William Armstrong and Charles Mitchell in their mansions in Jesmond to those of the inhabitants of the early industrial flats built at Garth Heads behind the Keelmen's Hospital or the workers of Pandon in their 'back-to-back' houses. Between 1869 and 1873 the average mortality rate in Newcastle was 282 per thousand, higher than that of any large provincial town except Liverpool and Manchester. Typhus was 'fearfully prevalent'. At an earlier date Palmerston had written of Newcastle's inhabitants, that they would 'see their neighbours perish around them and risk the lives of their wives and children and their own rather than ward off the dangers by arrangements which might involve a sixpenny rate'. Not until 1906 did the Newcastle corporation firmly shoulder responsibilities proposed by the Housing of the Working Classes Act of 1890 and lay out its first 'council estate' at Walker on a site of 16½ acres. Here the typical Tyneside terrace house of an upper and lower flat was built, 454 units in all, to be let at rentals varying from 2s 3d to 9s 3d a week.

MEDICINE

Tyneside offered great opportunities for the clinical study of medicine and surgery. Special attention could be paid to the incidence of industrial diseases, including the various forms of lead-poisoning and respiratory complaints. In 1876 the medical school at Newcastle proposed the institution of degrees in Sanitary Science, and in 1894 offered a Diploma of Public Health. The degrees of bachelor and doctor of hygiene were established in 1891. Bacteriological laboratories were established in 1895 and extended in 1923, because of heavy demands on their use for various public health purposes including the testing of milk for tuberculin infection. Clinical teaching is now distributed throughout the various Newcastle hospitals, which are integrated administratively with Newcastle University. Special attention is still devoted to the study of epidemics, the problems of general practice, and social medicine.

Provision for the sick and needy outside Newcastle was largely dependent on private benefactions. In Walker, Charles Mitchell helped to found the Walker Hospital for Accidents in 1870.

Previously many lives had been lost carrying accident patients to the Newcastle Infirmary. His shipyard workers agreed to contribute a halfpenny a week. In Wallsend the hospital is associated with Sir George Hunter, another shipbuilder. North Shields in 1888 added the Victoria Jubilee Infirmary for accidents, supported by voluntary subscriptions, to the facilities offered by the workhouse infirmary. At South Shields the infirmary was established as a testimonial of esteem to Robert Ingham, the town's member of parliament between 1832 and 1841, and between 1852 and 1868. Out of the total cost of £6,815, the Jarrow Chemical Company contributed £4,000, and the Dean and Chapter of Durham donated the site. The Ingham Infirmary was opened on 3 June 1873, and its income included regular weekly contributions paid by the men at the main local works, amounting to some £1,200, by virtue of which they were entitled to elect from themselves representatives on the governing body of the hospital. There was also a workhouse infirmary, and from 1882–3 an Infectious Diseases Hospital, since as a port, South Shields was liable to receive sailors infected with smallpox. In such an epidemic in 1870–1 over 373 people died. At Jarrow Sir Charles Mark Palmer founded in 1870 the Memorial Hospital, to which his workers contributed a penny a week from their pay. Gateshead Isolation Hospital dates from 1880. There was also a Children's Hospital and the workhouse infirmary.

POPULATION
Population on Tyneside had grown steadily throughout the nineteenth century, not only through natural causes but also by immigration. In 1874 the Newcastle Medical Officer of Health claimed that only Liverpool, Manchester and Bradford had a higher proportion of Irish in their population. In general, the Irish came as labourers and the Scots as craftsmen—particularly to the shipyards. The census returns provide statistics for the comparative growth of the different Tyneside communities. While Newcastle was by far the largest single authority on the Tyne, the proportion of its inhabitants to the total population of Tyne-

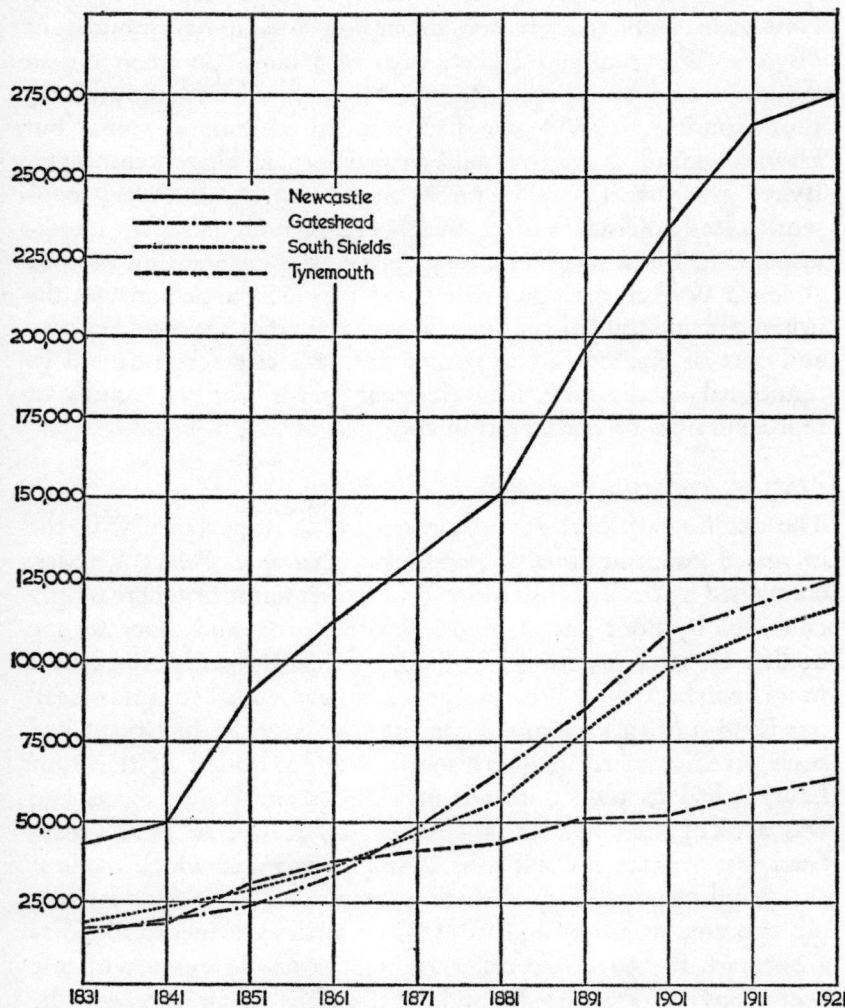

Fig 7a   The four County Boroughs of Tyneside: comparative populations

side declined from 43 per cent in 1851 to 36 per cent in 1921. In Newcastle itself the greatest expansion was in its suburbs of Elswick, Westgate and Byker, each of which was greater than the municipal and parliamentary borough of Tynemouth. By 1891 housing in Westgate had reached saturation point, but Elswick continued to grow with Armstrongs, its biggest employer. Byker grew with its ship-yards, engine-works, potteries, soap-works, lead smelting and chemicals. To provide itself with additional land for workers' housing, Newcastle corporation in 1904 annexed Walker, itself an urban district council, together with the urban district council of Benwell and the rural areas of Fenham and part of Kenton. At the same time the city reconstituted its traditional subdivisions into electoral wards, for the return of representatives on the city council.

LOCAL GOVERNMENT

The question of local government grew in importance with the increased concentration of people on Tyneside. Select Vestries, controlled by local industrialists, found their authority increasingly contested by Poor Law Unions, Health Boards and other ad hoc bodies. In 1835 Gateshead had been formally incorporated as a municipal borough. Previously it had owned a 'common seal' but had no other recognised corporate distinction. In 1834 it had been given a board of guardians for administration of the Poor Law. It had its own borough magistrates and police force, and was a recognised sanitary and school authority. In 1889 Gateshead was granted the status of County Borough, which made it also a highway authority. A similar story could be told for Jarrow, incorporated as a borough in 1875, or Wallsend, incorporated as a borough in 1901. The other authorities on Tyneside with the exceptions of Tynemouth and South Shields, all received the status of Urban District Councils in 1894, when the old Local Boards of Health were up-graded. Tynemouth had been incorporated as a borough in 1849 and South Shields in 1850, and both became County Boroughs in 1888.

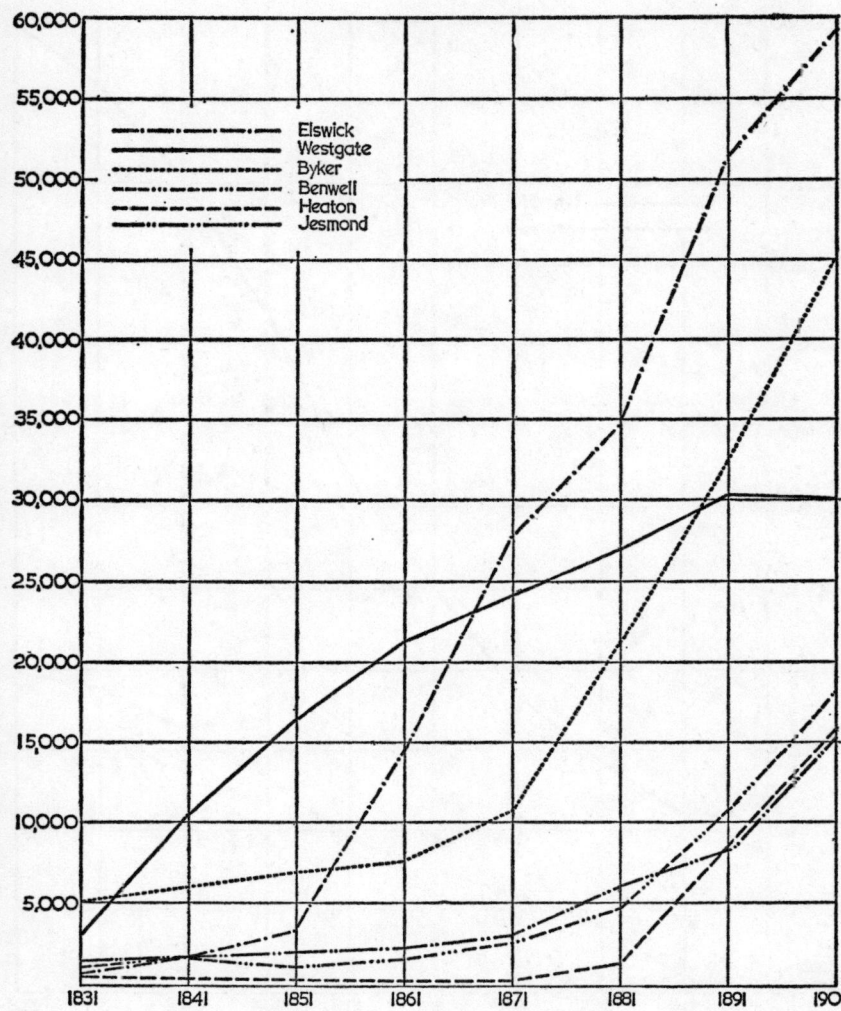

Fig 7b Comparative growth of population in the suburbs of Newcastle

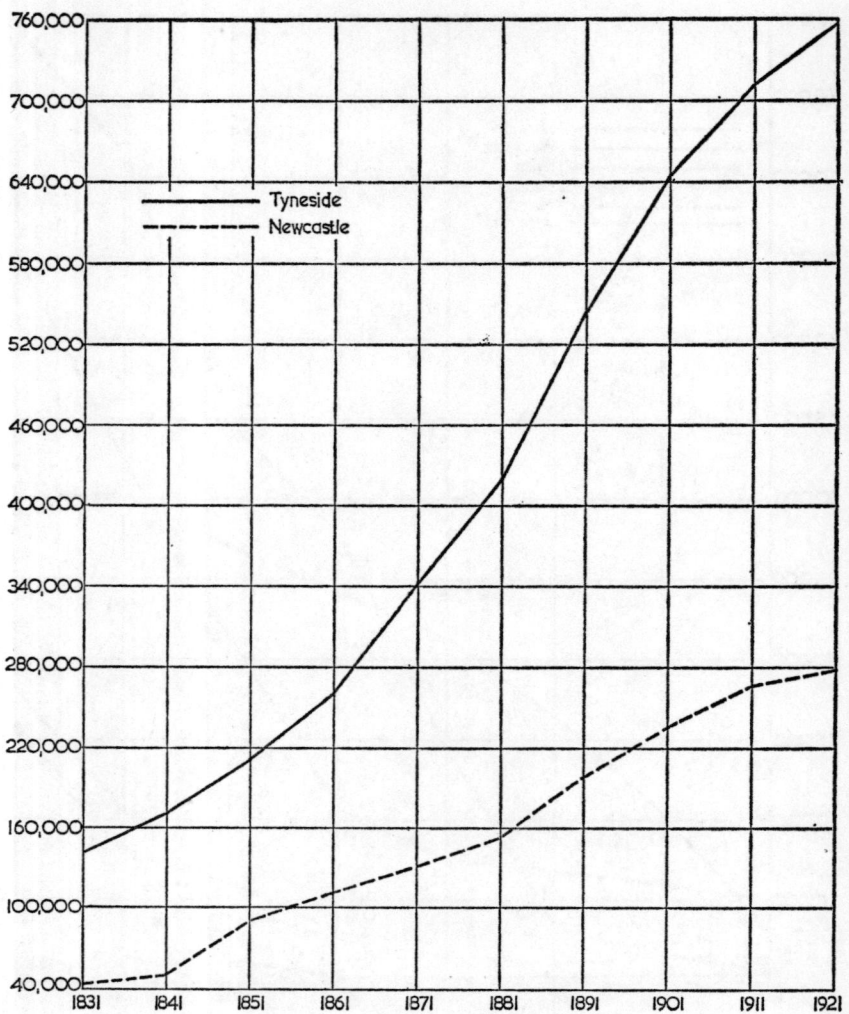

Fig 7c   Total population of Tyneside compared with Newcastle

AMENITIES

But man does not live a better life just because he has sewage disposal. What of Tyneside amenities? As early as the Health of Towns Commission in 1845, recommendations had been made for the provision of public walks. The Newcastle Town Moor was commended, except for its lack of tree shelter and the attentions of the freemen's cows. Gateshead had the remains of a common, known as the Windmill Hills from the number of mills nearby. North and South Shields had access to the seashore. In 1873 Dr Reid's suggestion to develop parts of the Town Moor as public parks was at last acted upon and Leazes Park was opened, followed in 1878 and 1880 by the Bull Park, where once the town bull had been stationed, and Brandling Park, adjacent to the Great North Road. Sir William Armstrong donated Armstrong Park in Heaton in 1880, followed by Jesmond Dene in 1883. West of the town, Elswick Hall was acquired by the corporation in 1878 and its grounds laid out as a public park. South Shields' Health Committee as early as 1855 considered the provision of a park, but deferred it because the cliff top and sea beach were already available, 'while the new cemetery of 16 acres, with a view of the sea, affords a quiet and pleasing retreat most conducive to health'. In 1867 the corporation leased a derelict brickyard between the old workhouse and the Sands, and laid it out as a recreation ground with swings and a pond for sailing model boats. In 1884 the corporation, to relieve current unemployment, levelled the old Ballast Hills and laid out the South Park; and by a similar use of unemployed labour (between 1893 and 1899) levelled the hills of salt waste to complete the North Park. West of the town there was a park adjacent to Tyne Dock. The eastern chain of parks constitute the main claim of South Shields to be a holiday resort. In Tynemouth, Spittal Dene was given by the duke of Northumberland as a park in 1885, the construction again providing work for the unemployed. The stretch of land opposite the old Aquarium, built in 1877–8, was leased from the duke for a second park in 1894. Wallsend received its parks largely

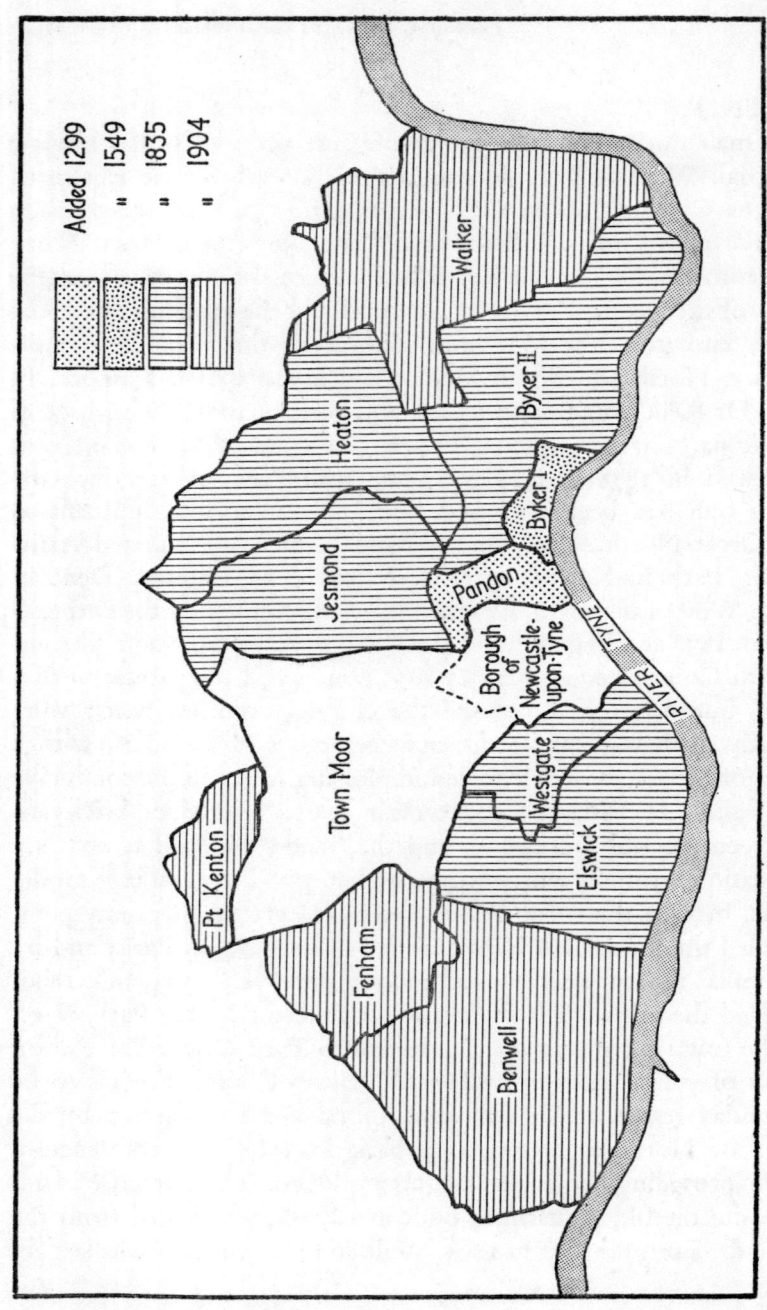

Fig 8 Growth of the boundaries of Newcastle

at the hands of Sir George Hunter, who between 1901 and 1914 bought various properties with grounds and presented them to the borough. Saltwell Park, Gateshead, is a memorial to those killed in the South African War (1899–1902).

For those wanting more excitement than a walk among the flowers, there were the traditional betting sports of 'Geordie bowling', where the contestants flung their clay balls and pursued them for a further cast, the winner covering the mile course with the fewest throws, and also skiff-racing on the river. The greatest of these oarsmen were 'Honest Bob' Chambers, who won the world sculling championship in 1863, and Harry Clasper, who won the Scottish championship in 1858. Horse-racing, originally held on Killingworth Moor, was transferred in 1721 to Newcastle Town Moor. The principal meeting was in Trinity Week, but as this date fluctuated with the church calendar it was altered to the week nearest to Midsummer Day (24 June). The first Northumberland Plate, the 'Pitmen's Derby', was run in 1833. In 1882 racing was transferred to Gosforth Park, but this was too distant for most of the poorer townsfolk. The North of England Temperance League rose to the opportunity and established on the Moor a Temperance Festival to coincide with Race Week, which has been continued to the present as the town 'hoppings' or fair. Blaydon Races, recorded for all time in 'Tyneside's National Anthem', were actually run only between 1861 and 1916. Organised football was late in becoming popular on Tyneside; when the Football League was formed in 1888, Newcastle had only two teams. Newcastle East End and Newcastle West End united in 1895 and acquired an intake of the Town Moor as a playing-field—St James' Park. Between 1904 and 1911 Newcastle United won the League championship three times, and captured the Cup in 1910.

Indoor entertainment was focused on theatres and music-halls. At the turn of the eighteenth century 'the North-Eastern Circuit' was run by the Kemble family, who managed theatres at North and South Shields as well as the Theatre Royal, Newcastle. By 1896 there were two theatres each at Newcastle, Gateshead and South Shields and one at North Shields. As for music halls, Newcastle had five and South Shields had two. Whereas the theatres provided spectacle and melodrama, the halls reflected everyday concerns, particularly those of the workers. The songs of Joe Wilson commemorated visiting notables but more especially the triumphs and defeats of Tyneside oarsmen, the pangs of new love, the friction between neighbours, matrimonial quarrels, the difficulties of housekeeping, and the dangers of drink.

In the course of the nineteenth century, life became a little easier for all. Working conditions and wages improved as employers realised that a healthy worker gave better service. Most important, however, the Tynesider had confidence in himself and faith in the future. Were not the Stephensons, Armstrong, Palmer, and even Parsons all fellow-workers who had grown rich on the river's industry?

SELECT BIBLIOGRAPHY

Census Returns, 1831–1921
Health of Town's Commission: report by D. B. Reid on the State of Newcastle-upon-Tyne and other Towns (1845)

W. RANGER	*Report to the General Board of Health . . . into . . . the Sanitary Condition of the Inhabitants of the Borough of Tynemouth* (1851)
E. ALLEN, J. F. CLARKE, N. McCORD and D. J. ROWE	*The North East Engineers' Strikes of 1871* (Newcastle, 1971)
R. J. CHARLTON	*A History of Newcastle upon Tyne* (no date)
N. LONGMATE	*King Cholera* (1966)
N. McCORD	'The Government of Tyneside, 1800–1850' *Transactions* of the Royal Historical Society, 5th Series XX, 1970)
F. MANDERS (ed)	*Bulletin* of the Gateshead and District Local History Society vol 1 pt 6 (1971)
F. W. ROGERS	'The Unreformed Borough of Gateshead' (*Arch Ael* 4th Series XLV, 1967) 'Gateshead and the Public Health Act of 1848' (*Arch Ael* 4th Series XLIX, 1971)
JOE WILSON	*Tyneside Songs and Drolleries* (Newcastle, 1890)

Chapter 9   SELF-HELP AND STATE
                INTERVENTION

PREVIOUS to 1914, Tyneside had experienced
confident prosperity. It had pioneered the use of coal, colliers
and railways for its own local purposes long before the Stephensons, Palmer and others had convinced the world it should look
to the Tyne for its needs. The early development on Tyneside
of electrical power for industrial uses merely underlined the fact
that local demand generated supply. The harnessing of British
industry to a total war-effort under governmental direction between
1915 and 1918 resulted on Tyneside in the loss of overseas customers. After the war these had found new sources of supply, or
learnt to produce for themselves.

INTER-WAR RECESSION
The war-years between 1914 and 1918 brought great financial
prosperity to the Tyne. Army and navy contracts filled the order-
books of the armaments empire of Armstrong, Whitworth at
Elswick and of the naval yards of Armstrong, Mitchell at Low
Walker, of Hawthorn, Leslie at Hebburn, and of Palmer at Jarrow.
With the end of World War I, pressure for production of armaments ceased whilst the returning soldiers and sailors looked for
their old employment. Tyneside had a greater diversity of ship-
yards than any similar region; but once the shipping losses from
enemy action were made good, there was no comparable volume
of later orders. Whereas in 1920 Swan, Hunters of Wallsend had
a building capacity of 170,000 gross tons, it built in 1923 only
41,000 tons of new ships. As Britain ceased to be the world's
workshop there was a decline in demand for sea-freight. Shipping

lines went bankrupt, and there was accumulated unemployment in all branches of the shipping world, including marine engineering and ship-repairing.

Discontent over wages and working-hours in the Northumberland and Durham coalfield contributed to the Coal Strike of 1926 which brought into high relief the precarious nature of employment on Tyneside, with its massive dependence on heavy industry. The first spectacular casualty was the Armstrong armaments empire. Following a disastrous attempt to diversify interests by building locomotives and then by embarking on a development scheme in Newfoundland, the insolvent company was forced to merge in 1928 with Vickers of Sheffield, henceforth to be known as Vickers, Armstrong. The great Palmer empire at Jarrow collapsed soon after. In 1931 Palmers had launched only one ship, and by late summer over 80 per cent of Jarrow's population were 'on the dole'. On 19 June 1932 HMS *Duchess*, the last of the long line of Palmers ships, was launched. Swan, Hunters, many times blue riband holders for the greatest shipbuilding firm in the world, received only six orders between April 1931 and April 1932, representing 16,000 tons. Hawthorn, Leslies reduced its work force from 5,004 in June 1931 to 1,049 in June 1933.

The National Shipbuilders Security Ltd was founded in 1930 to buy redundant or obsolete shipyards and to resell the sites for any industrial purpose except shipbuilding. (Government subsidies or interference in peace time were not welcomed.) By March 1932 nine Tyne yards had been purchased. In January 1933 it was estimated that 82·5 per cent of the Northern shipbuilding and ship-repair employees were out of work, against a national average of 63·5 per cent. Shipbuilding and marine engineering, moreover, were still the major employers. J. B. Priestley recorded in 1933 in his *English Journey* that 'wherever we went there were men hanging about, not scores of them but hundreds and thousands'. Palmers was bought by National Shipbuilders and shut down in 1934. Men were glad to be hired as ship-breakers or factory dismantlers. Archaeological excavation and public works were encouraged to provide work for the unemployed. Slowly, even the

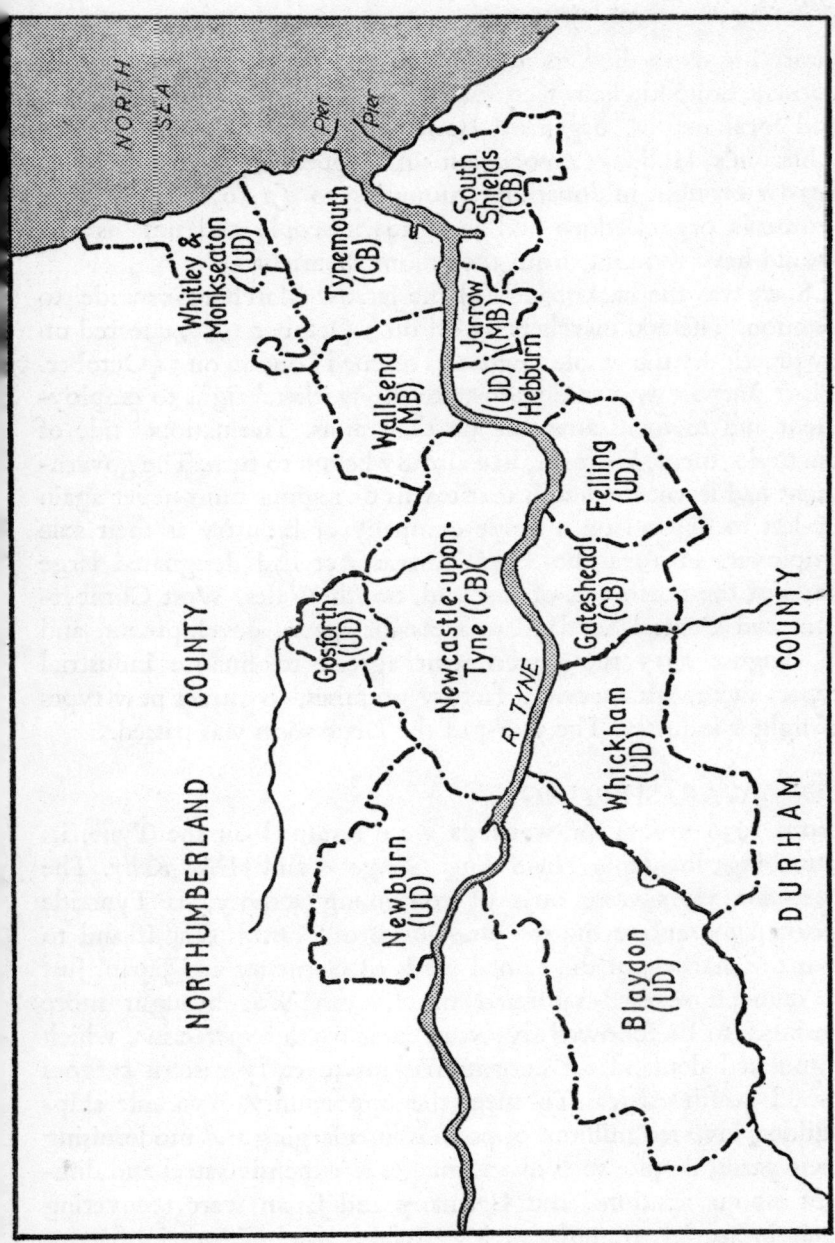

Fig 9 Boundaries of Local Government about 1928

I

desire for work died, as men and lads huddled listlessly at street-corners. Soup kitchens were established to feed the schoolchildren, and local mayors organised Boot and Shoe Funds or the Poor Children's Holiday Association. An appeal by the mayor of Jarrow brought in donations amounting to £1,567, mostly from women's organisations and local townspeople and not, as one would have thought, from the unions themselves.

Such was the background of the Jarrow March or 'crusade' to London. The 200 marchers set off on 5 October 1936, cheered on by practically the whole town, and reached London on 31 October. Their purpose was to demonstrate the workers' right to employment and to focus attention on their aims. The national tide of unemployment, however, had already begun to turn. The government had learnt the lesson that towns or regions must never again be left to depend on a single company or industry as their sole employer. In 1934 the Special Areas Act had designated large parts of the north-east of England, South Wales, West Cumberland and Central Scotland as areas for special development, and in August 1935 the government agreed to finance industrial estates there, with serviced factory premises, to attract new types of lighter industry. The worst of the Depression was passed.

POST-WAR SHIPPING

From 1936 orders for warships were resumed on the Tyne, its launchings including HMS *King George V* and HMS *Kelly*. The post-war years were ones of continuing activity, as Tyneside worked to replace the shipping losses of World War II and to win the markets of the ruined yards of Germany and Japan. Just as demand seemed saturated the Korean War brought more business, to be followed five years later by the Suez crisis, which stimulated demand for enormous ships to carry eastern cargoes round South Africa. To meet the opportunity, Tyneside shipbuilders invested millions of pounds in enlarging and modernising their yards, despite such disadvantages as expensive steel and difficult labour relations. But Germany and Japan were recovering their industrial strength, to give British shipbuilding its fiercest competition ever. Japan started to build huge tankers and took the lead as the world's principal shipbuilding nation, whilst the Tyneside ship-yards were handicapped by the restricted width of the river for launching purposes and by high overheads. The new 253,000 ton tankers built by Swan, Hunters cannot return to the Tyne for repairs once they have left the fitting-out quay at Wallsend.

POWER

Coal, the traditional source of Tyneside power and heating, has steadily declined in demand, and exports have fallen from 21 million tons in 1923 to under 3 million tons in 1971. Although World War II gave great stimulus to the demand for coal, competition from oil and natural gas has continued, so that only the most economic collieries remain in production. The last colliery on the north bank of the Tyne, the Rising Sun at Wallsend, closed in 1969. Only Westoe Colliery at South Shields is still in production. Tyneside power-stations, however, are fuelled by coal.

It should be noted that Reyrolles of Hebburn, who specialise in heavy electrical switchgear, was one of the few major Tyneside concerns to have a steady order-book during the 1930s. This was the period of the establishment of the Central Electricity Generating Board, which was one of its best customers.

INDUSTRIAL AND TRADING ESTATES

As a direct result of the inter-war trade depression, the need for government intervention became generally accepted. Tyneside was the first region to benefit from the Special Areas Act of 1934. The Team Valley Trading Estate to the south-west of Gateshead was established in 1936. Its object was to bring diversified light industry and also provide working opportunities for women. Hitherto there had been little choice for them but domestic service or the rope-works, where the brawny 'Haggie's Angels' were proverbial. It consists of 660 acres of land, most of which has been reclaimed from coal mining dereliction. Its range of products include mining machinery, clothing and textiles, steel furniture, electric delivery vehicles and small tools. Other such estates have been established since 1945. The Bede Industrial Estate at Jarrow has over twenty companies, employing 4,000 work-people, and produces ships' fittings, yarn, electrical goods, food, plastics and die castings. The West Chirton estate was formerly under the control of the borough of Tynemouth, being an early attempt to attract industries through municipal enterprise. The twenty firms on this estate employ over 4,000 workpeople in the manufacture of pneumatic tools, plastics, glassware, electroplating, precision tools, confectionery, knitwear and engineering equip-ment. Newburn estate is located upstream; its eight factories along the river bank being engaged in the processing of food and in the manufacture of engines, electrical batteries and earthmoving equip-ment. Other estates are at East Gateshead, Felling, Gosforth and the Tyne Tunnel.

Another way of providing employment is the decentralisation of government offices, and since 1948 the Department of Health and Social Security has had its records centre at Longbenton. This too is a massive employer of women's labour.

PLANNED DEVELOPMENT

The North East Development Council, with its headquarters at Newcastle upon Tyne, is primarily an organisation backed by central government and local planning authorities in north-east England to synchronise the needs of industry, trade unions and local government authorities and to promote trade with other regions and abroad. Yet another quasi-governmental agency is the Northern Economic Planning Council, also with its head-quarters at Newcastle upon Tyne. This is one of many regional councils set up by the government in 1964, and covers the counties of Northumberland, County Durham, the North Riding of Yorkshire, Cumberland and Westmorland. The objects of the Northern Council include the co-ordination of the activities of the departments of central government in the region. Private enter-prise has the Tyne and Wear Chamber of Commerce, formed in 1969 by the amalgamation of the Newcastle upon Tyne Chamber

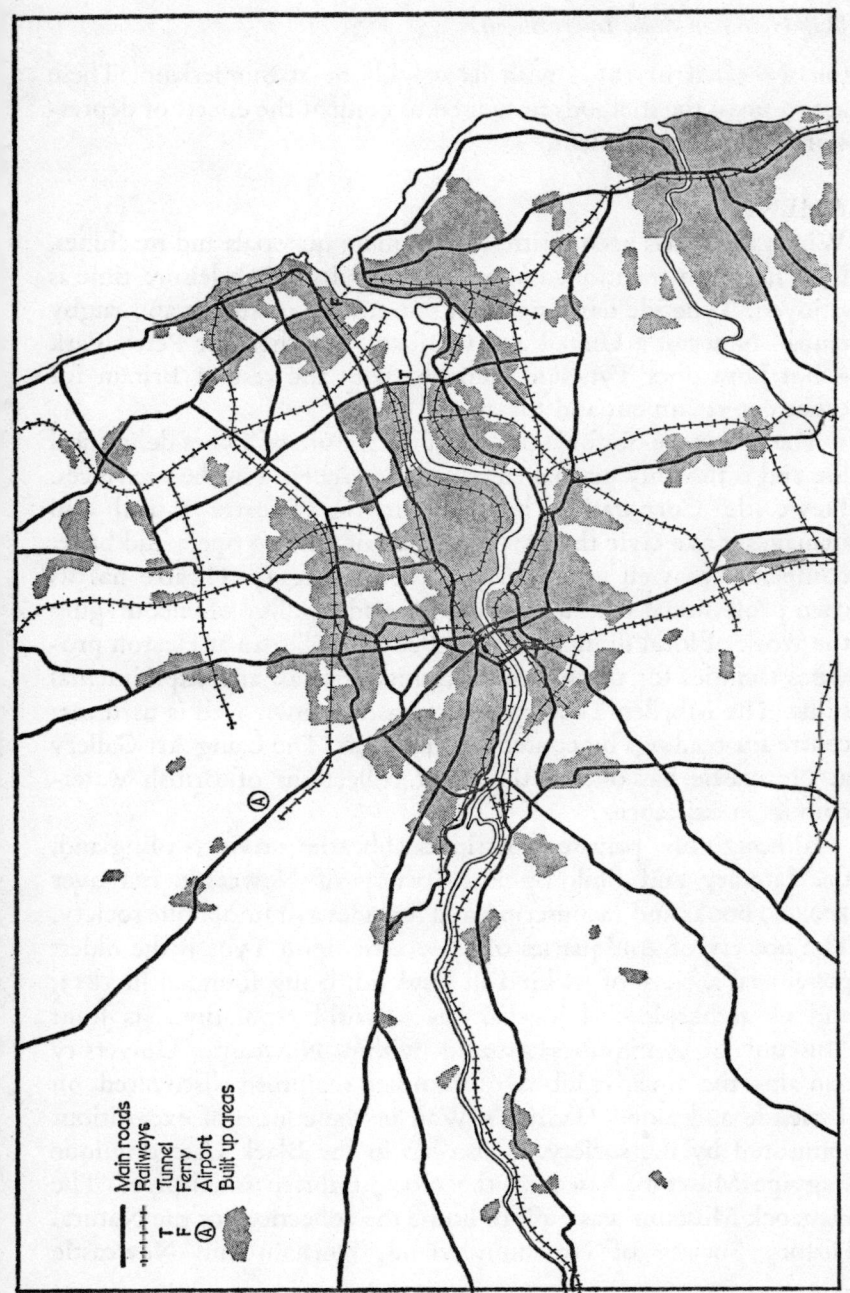

Fig 10 Modern communications

(incorporated in 1815) with its neighbour at Sunderland. These are some of the methods now used to combat the effects of depression and unemployment.

AMENITIES

Whilst much has been written about men, materials and machines, little has been mentioned about the way in which leisure time is enjoyed. Tyneside has long been famous for its soccer and rugby clubs—Newcastle United and Gosforth, Northern or Percy Park —but how does Tyneside compare with the rest of Britain for other entertainment and the arts?

The Northern Sinfonia orchestra is a feature of Tyneside musical life and is the only permanent chamber orchestra in the provinces. Newcastle Corporation has bought the Theatre Royal and manages it as a civic theatre for the use of visiting opera and ballet companies as well as for plays. The University Theatre has its own professional repertory company and a policy of encouraging the work of local dramatists. The People's Theatre at Heaton provides facilities for theatre clubs, musical recitals and experimental films. The Morden Tower on Newcastle's town wall is used as a centre for readings by contemporary poets. The Laing Art Gallery at Newcastle has one of the finest collections of British water-colours in existence.

Although few private subscription libraries survive in England, the Literary and Philosophical Society of Newcastle has over 100,000 books and manuscripts and includes a gramophone society. The Society of Antiquaries of Newcastle upon Tyne is the oldest provincial society of its kind in England, being founded in 1813, and its archaeological journal has a world reputation. Its Joint Museum of Antiquities situated within Newcastle University contains the finer exhibits of Roman sculpture discovered on Tyneside and along Hadrian's Wall in the course of excavations sponsored by the society. It also has in the Black Gate a unique Bagpipe Museum, based on the Northumbrian small-pipes. The Hancock Museum was built to house the collections of the Natural History Society of Northumberland, Durham and Newcastle upon Tyne, based on the work of two distinguished brother naturalists, Albany and John Hancock. A new folk museum, named after its benefactor John George Joicey, has been opened in the ancient Holy Jesus Hospital. *Turbinia* is displayed in the Museum of Science and Engineering situated on the Newcastle Town Moor.

Tyneside stands poised on the brink of the fourth quarter of the twentieth century. Its future is bound up with the local government bill which proposes in 1974 to link Wearside with Tyneside in a new metropolitan county. But Tynesiders have a fierce pride of identity, which they are reluctant to merge. They remember the important role of the Tyne in the industrial revolution of the nineteenth century.

The unique nature, however, of Tyneside lies in the continuity of its industrial history. From the fourteenth century its prosperity has been dependent on the coal trade and its ancillary services. Now that coal is no longer the mainstay of British industry a very real question-mark hangs over Tyneside's future. Already it is proposed that a Minister of the North be appointed with special responsibility for trade expansion. Newcastle is the focal point of communications in the north east and has long been its financial capital, with its banking facilities. It remains to be seen if it can offer comparable services with its university, polytechnic and research institutions, and its skilled manpower.

SELECT BIBLIOGRAPHY

P. J. Bowden and A. A. Gibb	'Economic Development in the Twentieth Century' (*Durham County and City with Teeside*: British Association, 1970)
J. M. Cousins and R. K. Brown	'Shipbuilding in the North East' (*Durham County . . .*, Brit Ass, 1970)
J. W. House	*Industrial Britain: the North East* (Newton Abbot, 1969)
H. A. Mess	*Industrial Tyneside: a Social Survey* (1928)
W. Reid	'The Coal Mining Industry' (*Durham County . . .*, Brit Ass, 1970)

GENERAL BIBLIOGRAPHY

W. G. ARMSTRONG (ed), *The Industrial Resources of the Tyne, Wear and Tees* (2nd ed 1864)

J. BRAND, *History of Newcastle upon Tyne*, 2 vols (Newcastle, 1789)

T. CRAWFORD, *Nineteenth Century Notes on Walker* (Newcastle, 1904)

F. W. DENDY (ed), *Newcastle Merchant Adventurers* (Surtees Soc 93, 101 for 1894, 1899)

D. J. DOUGAN, *The History of North East Shipbuilding* (1968)

G. HODGSON, *The Borough of South Shields* (Newcastle, 1903)

R. HOWELL, JR, *Newcastle-upon-Tyne and the Puritan Revolution* (Oxford, 1967)

E. HUGHES, *North Country Life in the Eighteenth Century*, i (Oxford, 1952)

E. MACKENZIE, *History of Newcastle* (1827)

S. MIDDLEBROOK, *Newcastle upon Tyne: its Growth and Achievement* (Newcastle, 1950)

J. U. NEF, *The Rise of the British Coal Industry*, 2 vols (1932; reprinted 1966)
Northumberland County History VIII, XIII (1907, 1930)

W. RICHARDSON, *History of the Parish of Wallsend* (Newcastle, 1923)

J. D. SCOTT, *Vickers: a History* (1962)

J. SYKES, *Local Records*, 3 vols (Newcastle, new edition, 1866-7)

R. WELFORD, *History of Newcastle and Gateshead*, 3 vols (1884-7)

R. WELFORD, *Men of Mark 'Twixt Tyne and Tweed*, 3 vols (1895)

C. E. WHITING, *The University of Durham, 1832-1932* (1932)

INDEX